IMAGES
of America

TENNESSEE'S CONFEDERATES

Cumberland College first offered classes in 1789. The appointment of Rev. Phillip Lindsley as chancellor in 1824 precipitated a name change to the University of Nashville. Under Lindsley's son John Berrien, the University of Nashville merged with the Western Military Institute in 1855 and adopted a military curriculum. Many Confederate soldiers and political leaders attended the school or taught within its halls, including Gideon Pillow, William Barksdale, George Maney, Sam Davis, Thomas Benton Smith, and Bushrod Johnson. This photograph shows Lindsley Hall during the Union occupation of Nashville. Vanderbilt University and Montgomery Bell Academy trace their beginnings to the University of Nashville. (Courtesy of the Library of Congress.)

ON THE COVER: Confederate veterans of Nashville's Nathan Bedford Forrest Camp, Troop A, are shown attending the National Confederate Veterans Reunion in Washington, D.C., in 1917. (Courtesy of the Library of Congress.)

IMAGES
of America

TENNESSEE'S
CONFEDERATES

Myers E. Brown II
with the Tennessee State Museum

ARCADIA
PUBLISHING

Published by Arcadia Publishing
Charleston, South Carolina

Printed in the United States of America

Library of Congress Control Number: 2010934494

For all general information, please contact Arcadia Publishing:
Telephone 843-853-2070
Fax 843-853-0044
E-mail sales@arcadiapublishing.com
For customer service and orders:
Toll-Free 1-888-313-2665

Visit us on the Internet at www.arcadiapublishing.com

To the memory of Tennessee's Confederates—may your bravery, suffering, and actions be remembered for another 150 years.

CONTENTS

ACKNOWLEDGMENTS

First and foremost, I would like to acknowledge Jesus Christ, our Lord and Savior, for the blessings he continues to bestow upon my family and me.

Many people have contributed their time, talents, efforts, and collections to assist me in this endeavor. I certainly could not have accomplished this work without the help of the following people: my coworkers at the Tennessee State Museum, specifically Mick Morin, Brad Kavan, and Bob White; Karina McDaniel, Amber Gilmer, and Carol White of the Tennessee State Library and Archives; Anne Toplovich and Kelly Wilkerson of the Tennessee Historical Society; Michelle and Dan McDonald of the East Tennessee History Center; Judy Duke and Pam Philpot of the Cookeville Museum of History; Joanna Stephens of the Battle of Franklin Trust; Norma Steele of the Paris–Henry County Museum; Tony Guzzi of the Hermitage; Ephraim J. Rotter of the Thomasville, Georgia, Historical Society; Retha Stephens and Clay Melvin of Kennesaw Mountain National Military Park; the Alabama Department of Archives and History; and Pat Meguiar, Ken Thomsen, Dr. Sam Barnes, David Sullivan, Thomas Hammock, Ramsey Powell, Ronnie Mangrum, and Robert L. Parker. Americans are blessed with the Library of Congress's digitized photographic collection. Some of these images are utilized here.

Ronnie Townes has an incredible collection of Tennessee Civil War images. Ronnie made his collection available to me for this book. Images of America: *Tennessee's Confederates* would not have been possible without access to his collection. Other private collectors also made their collections available to me. A special thank you to the following: Dr. Anthony Hodges, Daniel J. Taylor, and Bruce Holher. All of these men are true Southern gentlemen. I am honored to know them and honored that they trusted me with their images. I owe them a debt of gratitude.

The folks at Arcadia, especially my editor Maggie Bullwinkel, should be thanked as well. Maggie has kept me on task and has worked through my tardiness and numerous changes in photographs and text.

Lastly, I would like to thank my family, especially my wife, Angie, and daughter, Morgan While I have worked on this volume, you continued to tolerate my irascible moods and forgave my neglect of other things. Thank you and I love you both more than I ever express.

INTRODUCTION

Gov. William Bowen Campbell pointed out in his inauguration speech in 1851 that Tennessee was perfectly juxtaposed between the grain belt of the Midwestern states and the cotton belt of the Southeastern states and was blessed with rivers that connected the two sections. He also advocated the construction of rail lines across the state to strengthen the state's economic position. While the geographic location of the state was and continues to be a blessing for Tennessee, it also placed the state in a position to be a major battleground with the outbreak of the Civil War. In fact, there was not a community within the state that did not bear witness to some type of armed conflict. Tennessee's physical location within the Union was not lost on the leaders of the period.

Tennesseans worked diligently for over a decade to avoid armed conflict between the North and South. With the growth of slavery consuming the nation in the aftermath of the Mexican War, delegates from across the South, especially Tennessee, met in Nashville in 1850. These delegates hammered out the beginnings of a compromise that eventually made its way to the floors of Congress and became the Compromise of 1850. These efforts held off the war for a decade. Even in the watershed presidential election of 1860, Tennessee strove for compromise to avoid war. Tennessean John Bell ran on a platform to preserve the Union and to adhere to the Constitution, which protected slavery. Bell's Constitutional Union Party carried Tennessee, Kentucky, and Virginia. Despite this fact, Abraham Lincoln won the election and triggered secession by South Carolina, followed by all of the Deep South states. Despite the efforts of the pro-secessionist Gov. Isham Harris, Tennesseans rejected secession and hoped for a peaceful resolution to the crisis.

The Confederate attack on Fort Sumter in Charleston, South Carolina, changed the stance of many Tennesseans. With the attack on Fort Sumter, President Lincoln called for each state to provide troops to put down the rebellion. Governor Harris telegraphed Lincoln the following: "Tennessee will not furnish a single man for the purpose of coercion, but 50,000 if necessary for the defense of our rights and those of our Southern brothers." Harris encouraged the General Assembly to hold a secession convention to be held in June. In the meantime, Tennessee entered into a military alliance with the Confederate states and began to organize an army. The mood of the state changed dramatically in a few short months. The June 8 referendum on secession was decisive—102,172 for secession and 47,238 for remaining with the Union. Tennessee cast her lot with the Confederacy, despite almost a third of the state being opposed.

Thousands of young men flocked to enlist in cavalry battalions, infantry regiments, and artillery batteries. Meanwhile, state and Confederate military leaders looked to constructing defenses along the Mississippi, Tennessee, and Cumberland Rivers and along the Kentucky border.

These rivers and the railroads that crisscrossed the state, advantages in times of peace, proved to be superhighways for invading armies. Nashville, Memphis, and most of Middle and West Tennessee fell to Union forces by the middle of 1863. Pro-Union East Tennessee fell to Union forces by the end of 1863. While the Confederates raided into Tennessee, launched campaigns

7

into the state, and even held small pockets of the state at various times, by the end of 1864, Union troops held sway. For much of the war, Tennessee's valuable natural resources, agricultural products, manufacturing facilities, and transportation centers remained unavailable to the Confederacy.

Ultimately, Tennessee provided nearly 187, 000 men to the Confederate armies, many thousands more than pledged by Governor Harris. The vast majority of these men served in either the Army of Tennessee or the Army of Mississippi. These two armies, often fighting in conjunction, had the responsibility of defending Tennessee, Mississippi, Alabama, portions of Louisiana, and Georgia. By 1865, they had fought also in Missouri, Kentucky, Virginia, and the Carolinas. These men experienced few victories but fought in some of the most decisive battles of the war—Fort Donelson, Shiloh, Perryville, Murfreesboro, Chickamauga, Chattanooga, Vicksburg, Atlanta, Franklin, and Nashville.

While the majority of Tennessee troops fought in the Western theater, three regiments served the entire war in the Army of Northern Virginia, and they would be joined by other Tennessee regiments in 1864. These units fought at places like Seven Pines, Second Manassas, Chancellorsville, Sharpsburg, Fredericksburg, Gettysburg, the Wilderness, Spotsylvania, Petersburg, and Richmond. Ultimately, Tennesseans (either as individuals or as units) served in every major Confederate army. Thousands died, and even more returned to Tennessee with broken bodies and in poor health.

Tennessee was the last state to leave the Union and the first state to return; yet the state still suffered through the difficulties of a Reconstruction plan administered by a particularly vindictive Tennessee Unionist in the form of Gov. William G. Brownlow.

When Tennessee's Confederates returned home, they found their state transformed in their absence. Continual campaigning, Union occupation, and violent guerrilla warfare left the state in ruins, and the Union victory and Reconstruction freed slaves and upturned the prewar social, economic, and political order. Returning soldiers struggled to reestablish their lives and process their experiences. Some never recovered, while others prospered and rose to political prominence. Regardless, the war proved to be the defining event of their lives and the watershed event in Tennessee and American history.

This volume only begins to tell the story of these men. There are many more stories to be told. For brevity, the following abbreviations are used in the credit lines: TSM–Tennessee State Museum; TSLA–Tennessee State Library and Archives; and LOC–Library of Congress. The collections of the Tennessee Historical Society reside at either the Tennessee State Museum or the Tennessee State Library and Archives. Their collections are identified as THS. Also for brevity, I often omitted the designation "Cavalry" or "Infantry," as these units are in segregated chapters. In order to include as many images as possible, I have omitted an index and a bibliography. Generally speaking, brigadier generals are in alphabetical order, preceded by major generals and lieutenant generals. Other chapters are in regimental numeric order with officers listed first, followed by enlisted men. Sources consulted include: the compiled service records of the Confederate Army; *Generals in Gray; Tennesseans in the Civil War, Volumes I and II; The Biographical Directory of the Tennessee General Assembly; Hancock's Diary: A History of the 2nd Tennessee Cavalry; The Tennessee Encyclopedia of History and Culture; Biographical Sketches of the Commissioned Officers of the Confederate States Marine Corps; Company Aytch, Revised and Expanded Edition;* and *Portrait of Conflict: Tennessee.*

One

THE POLITICAL LEADERS

Tennessee's political leaders reflected the views of many of their constituents and were divided over the issue of secession. When other Southern states left the Union, some of the Tennessee delegation in Washington simply withdrew from the political arena, while others diligently worked to prevent secession and the war. Unclear of how to proceed in this situation, Sen. Alfred Nicholson simply stopped attending sessions. Meanwhile, Tennessee governor Isham Harris sought unofficial alliances with the seceded states and encouraged the creation of military companies. Initially, the state rejected secession, and many Tennesseans hoped that a compromise could be reached. Indeed, many of Tennessee's leaders actively participated in the Nashville Convention over a decade before, which resulted in the Compromise of 1850.

On April 12, 1861, Confederate forces fired on Fort Sumter. President Lincoln's call for troops to put down the rebellion pushed Tennessee to secession. Governor Harris and the legislature declared the state independent in May and called for a public referendum in June. In the interim, Tennessee remained an independent entity with a provisional army and entered into an alliance with the Confederate States of America. The June referendum confirmed the legislature's actions, and Tennessee joined the Confederacy. Most political leaders sided with their constituents and continued their careers in either the General Assembly or in the Confederate Congress. Tennessee's Confederate senators carried decades of political experience to Richmond, especially in the form of Gustavus Henry of Clarksville. Meanwhile, perhaps in an attempt to pacify the East Tennessee Unionists, the state legislature sent Landon Carter Haynes of Johnson City to fill the other Senate seat.

While some of the political leaders shirked military duty and even abandoned their political posts, others joined military commands. Often blamed for leading the state into secession, Isham Harris volunteered as an aide-de-camp (camp assistant) to several Confederate generals and was even present at the death of Albert Sidney Johnston at Shiloh. Others gave up politics entirely and dedicated their energies to the military struggle. Regardless, all of them suffered for their decisions after the state fell to Union forces.

JOHN BELL, in a recent secession speech at Knoxville, said, "For himself he had taken his position. The noose was probably around his neck, but he was frank to declare himself a rebel!"

John Bell ranked among the preeminent antebellum Whig politicians. Born in Davidson County, he practiced law and served in the Tennessee Senate and House. Elected to the U.S. Congress in 1827, he served as Speaker of the House in 1834 and as Secretary of War under Pres. William Henry Harrison. Bell formed the Constitutional Union Party and ran for president in 1860 with a platform dedicated to the preservation of slavery and the Union. He carried the following three states in the election: Tennessee, Kentucky, and Virginia. Bell's success reflected the thoughts of many Tennesseans. With Tennessee's secession, Bell followed his state, although he took no active role in the new Confederate government. He died at his home in Stewart County in 1869. The image on the left is an envelope bearing the quote in regards to Bell joining the Confederate cause. The image below shows Bell before the war. (Left, TSM; below, LOC.)

Born near Tullahoma in 1818, Isham Harris moved at age 14 to Paris, Henry County, Tennessee. There he worked as a clerk and practiced law before moving to Memphis in 1853. Harris was active in Democratic politics and served in the General Assembly and the House of Representatives throughout the 1840s and early 1850s. Elected governor in 1857, Harris became the leader of the pro-secession movement in Tennessee and responded to Lincoln's call for troops with the bold statement, 'Tennessee will not furnish a single man for the purpose of coercion, but 50,000 if necessary for the defense of our rights and those of our Southern brothers." The fall of most of Tennessee to Union forces left Harris as governor in name alone. He served as a volunteer aid to several Confederate generals and was alongside Albert Sidney Johnston when that general received his death wound at Shiloh. After the war, Harris fled to Mexico and England but returned to Memphis in 1867. He served in the U.S. Senate from 1877 until his death in Washington, D.C., in 1897. (LOC.)

Alfred Osborne Pope Nicholson represented Maury County in the General Assembly as a Democrat. He supported Andrew Johnson for governor and served alongside him in the U.S. Senate until Tennessee seceded. Nicholson played no major role in the Confederate government and attempted to return home in 1864, only to be arrested. Pardoned for his actions in 1865, Nicholson served as chief justice of the Tennessee Supreme Court from 1870 until his death in 1876. (LOC.)

Alfred Osborne Pope Nicholson, editor of the *Daily Union*, supported Andrew Johnson for governor in the election of 1853 and presented him a cased set of pepperbox pistols at his inauguration. This photograph is a detail of the inscription. Ironically, Johnson ordered Nicholson arrested when he attempted to return to Tennessee in 1864. As president, Johnson issued a pardon for Nicholson's actions in 1865. (TSM.)

Gustavus Henry served as one of Tennessee's two Confederate senators and carried the moniker "the Eagle Orator of Tennessee." Born in Kentucky, Henry was a prominent Whig politician in his native state. He married Marion McClure in 1833 and moved to Clarksville, where he worked as an attorney and in the insurance business before his election to the General Assembly in 1851. Governor Harris appointed Henry as a commissioner to enter into a military league with the Confederate States before his election as senator. After the war, he joined the Democratic Party and in 1874 was chairman of the state convention. He died in 1880 and was buried in Greenwood Cemetery in Clarksville. (Emily and Ronnie Townes.)

Born near Elizabethton in 1816, Landon Carter Haynes attended Washington College and worked as an attorney in Jonesboro and Elizabethton. He lived on the historic Tipton farm near Johnson City. Haynes, a Democrat and an eloquent speaker, was involved with several confrontations with the equally vocal Whig editor William Brownlow, one of which resulted in Brownlow receiving a gunshot wound. Haynes served in the General Assembly throughout the 1840s and 1850s and as a presidential elector for James K. Polk and later for John C. Breckenridge. Defying many of his constituents, Haynes supported secession and joined Gustavus Henry as Tennessee's two Confederate senators. Haynes feared for his life due to his pro-Confederate stance in an area dominated by Unionists and relocated to Memphis after the war. There he died in 1875. His home in Johnson City is a state historic site. (TSLA.)

Henry Stuart Foote helped found LaGrange College in Alabama and served as senator and governor in Mississippi before settling in Nashville in 1859. A Unionist, Foote reluctantly supported secession and represented Nashville in the Confederate House of Representatives, where he obnoxiously opposed his old rival Jefferson Davis. He fled to the North in 1865, which resulted in his expulsion from Congress. He eventually fled to Canada and returned to Nashville in 1867. (LOC.)

A native of Henry County, John DeWitt Clinton Atkins served in the Tennessee General Assembly as a Democrat before serving in the U.S. House of Representatives from 1857 to 1859. Atkins supported John C. Breckenridge for president in 1860. After secession, he briefly served as lieutenant colonel of the 5th Tennessee Infantry. He resigned to serve in the Confederate Congress, a position he held until the end of the war. (LOC.)

George Washington Barrow was born in Nashville in 1808 and graduated from the University o
Nashville. He passed the bar in 1827 and married Anna Marrian Shelby. Barrow served in the
Seminole War, was active in Whig politics, and served as the minister to Portugal. Elected to
Congress in 1847, Barrow joined the opposition to the Mexican War led by Abraham Lincoln
which spelled his defeat in 1849. He was a member of the Nashville Convention, which laid the
groundwork for the Compromise of 1850, and he was the founder of the Nashville Gas Ligh
Company. Embracing secession, he pushed for Tennessee's secret alliance with the Confederac
prior to the state's secession. He raised and equipped the "Barrow Guards," which became Compan
C, 11th Tennessee Cavalry. He was arrested for treason by Andrew Johnson, refused to take the
oath of allegiance, and was not exchanged until 1863. He unsuccessfully ran for Confederat
governor and spent the remainder of the war as a private in the 50th Tennessee Infantry. Afte
the war, he returned to Nashville in poor health and financially ruined. He died within th
year. (TSLA.)

Born near Franklin in 1827, John Ford House represented Montgomery County in the General Assembly. House served in the Confederate Congress and as a volunteer aide-de-camp to Gen. George Maney in the Army of Tennessee. He was recalled to Richmond in May 1864 to serve as judge advocate in a cavalry command. After the war, he served in Congress until 1883. He died in Clarksville in 1904. (LOC.)

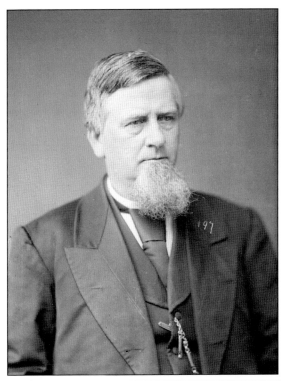

Michael Walsh Cluskey served as the postmaster of the U.S. House of Representatives from 1857 to 1859, and this sketch by the artist Alfred Waud was done at that time. Cluskey served as a staff officer for the following Tennessee generals during the war: William Bate, Preston Smith, Alfred Vaughn, and George Gordon. He resigned from the army in 1864 to represent Tennessee in the Confederate House of Representatives. (LOC.)

Thomas M. Jones moved to Giles County at age two. He attended the University of Alabama and the University of Virginia, practiced law in Pulaski, and served in the Seminole War. Active in politics, he served as the mayor of Pulaski, in the Tennessee General Assembly, and in the Provisional Confederate Congress until early in 1862. After the war, he returned to his law practice and served as a judge. He is credited as the founder of the Ku Klux Klan and was a Master Mason and a Knight Templar. He appeared for this photograph with his Masonic regalia. (TSLA.)

Two

TENNESSEE'S GENERALS

Tennessee received credit for providing 40 generals to the Confederacy, with a breakdown as follows: 2 lieutenant generals, 8 major generals, and 30 brigadier generals. However, many generals credited to other Southern states called Tennessee home. William Barksdale, a native of Rutherford County, later moved to Mississippi. Other sons of the Volunteer State relocated in the antebellum period. Ben McCulloch, for example, moved to Texas with his friend David Crockett in the 1830s and achieved fame as a Texas Ranger and as a Confederate general, though he too was a native of Rutherford County. Tennessee's influence on the Confederate high command thus extended beyond the number of generals actually credited to the state. Likewise, Tennessee claimed many generals native to other states. For example, three Tennessee generals called Ohio their native state. Included in this chapter are images of many of the generals credited to Tennessee, as well as those born in Tennessee.

Regardless of their nativity, the prewar military experiences of Tennessee's generals varied greatly. Generals such as Cadmus Wilcox and A. P. Stewart benefitted from U.S. Military Academy educations. Others, such as Felix Zollicoffer and Frank Cheatham, received military experience in the Seminole and Mexican Wars, while Thomas Benton Smith and George Washington Gordon attended private military schools before the war.

Prior military experience did not necessarily ensure success in the Confederate army. John McCown, cited for gallantry in the Mexican War, suffered through an embarrassing court martial and reduction in rank. Gideon Pillow, the ranking general in the Provisional Army of Tennessee and a Mexican War veteran, failed at Fort Donelson and thus never rose above brigadier general after Tennessee joined the Confederacy. Meanwhile, Gen. Nathan Bedford Forrest benefitted from neither prior military experience nor much formal education, yet he proved to be one of the most successful commanders produced by either side during the war.

Regardless of the success or failures of these generals, almost to the man, they risked everything to side with the Confederacy. Many would lose their lives, their fortunes, their freedom, their families, and their health as a result of their wartime service.

Gideon Pillow served as major general in the Mexican War, a commission he received due to his relationship with President Polk. Upon secession, Pillow was the ranking officer of the Provisional Army of Tennessee. Inept leadership at Fort Donelson overshadowed his role in organizing and equipping the Tennessee troops in 1861, and he held only minor commands after 1862. He practiced law after the war with Isham Harris (page 11) in Memphis. (TSM.)

A native of Sevierville, John Porter McCown served for 16 years in the regular army. With Tennessee's secession, he resigned his commission and commanded the defenses around New Madrid and Island No. 10. Blamed for the Confederate defeat, McCown's reputation suffered. Gen. Braxton Bragg charged him with disobedience at Stones River, and a court martial found him guilty. He remained in obscurity for the rest of the war. After the war, he taught school in Knoxville but later moved to Arkansas. (East Tennessee History Center, Knoxville, photograph by Dan McDonald.)

Daniel Smith Donelson's lineage included some of the earliest and most prominent families in Middle Tennessee. Born in Sumner County, he graduated from the U.S. Military Academy in 1825 but resigned in 1828. A planter by occupation, Donelson was also active in politics and served as Speaker of the Tennessee House of Representatives. Donelson ardently supported secession and received an appointment as brigadier general of state troops. As such, he selected the site for the Cumberland River defenses that bore his name (Fort Donelson). He served in Virginia and South Carolina before joining the Army of Tennessee in 1862. His brigade successfully assaulted the Union lines at Perryville and Murfreesboro, which resulted in his promotion to major general. Congress confirmed his promotion only days after his death by disease on April 17, 1863. (Emily and Ronnie Townes.)

After Tennessee joined the Confederacy, Gen. Leonidas Polk, who was a bishop prior to the war, commanded the Mississippi River defenses and established his headquarters in Memphis. Polk was no stranger to Tennessee. Born in North Carolina and a graduate of the U.S. Military Academy, Polk moved to Maury County in 1832 and served in the Episcopal ministry, eventually becoming the bishop of Louisiana. Bishop Polk was a strong proponent of education and helped establish the University of the South at Sewanee in 1860. A close associate of Jefferson Davis, Polk's rank outclassed his abilities; however, he commanded the Department of Alabama and a corps in the Army of Tennessee. He fought with the Army of Tennessee until killed by Union artillery at Pine Mountain, Georgia, in 1864. The left image depicts Polk in his Episcopal robes, while the image below shows Polk early in the war as a general. (Both, LOC.)

Born in Rogersville, Alexander Peter Stewart graduated from the U.S. Military Academy but resigned to teach school at Cumberland University in Lebanon and the University of Nashville. Stewart commanded artillery early in the war and ultimately an infantry corps in the Army of Tennessee. After the war, Stewart returned to Cumberland University, owned a business, and finally served as the chancellor of the University of Mississippi. He was also active in the Tennessee Historical Society and a commissioner of the Chickamauga-Chattanooga National Military Park. The noted Civil War artist Alfred Waud created this sketch of General Stewart. (LOC.)

The most successful cavalry commander of the war, Nathan Bedford Forrest, struck fear in the hearts of Union commanders. This Bedford County native moved to Memphis and became one of the wealthiest men of the city before the war. Enlisting as a private, Forrest received a discharge and recruited and equipped his own battalion of cavalry. Forrest's natural abilities and leadership skills made him a fearsome independent commander, although he often clashed with his superiors. His successes led to promotions, and he commanded cavalry for the entire war. He received promotion to lieutenant general in 1865, thus joining A. P. Stewart as the only native born Tennesseans to attain this rank. Forrest remains one of the most controversial figures in American history due to the Battle of Fort Pillow and his service as the grand wizard of the Ku Klux Klan, despite the fact that he dissolved the organization in 1869. (LOC.)

Born in Nashville, Benjamin Franklin Cheatham served as a captain in the "Bloody First" Tennessee during the Mexican War and later served as colonel of the 3rd Tennessee Infantry. After the Mexican War, Cheatham sought his fortune in the California Gold Rush only to find that operating a saloon for the miners was more profitable. He returned to Nashville in 1853. Cheatham's Mexican War experience earned him the command of a brigade of Tennessee troops after secession. He served with distinction in nearly every battle of the Western theater and eventually commanded a corps in the Tennessee Campaign of 1864. After the war, Cheatham served as the superintendent of the state penitentiary and as postmaster of Nashville and provided endorsements for Lem Motlow's Tennessee Whiskey. He is buried in Mount Olivet Cemetery in Nashville. The right image shows Cheatham early in the war, and the image below is a photograph from later in the war. (Right, TSM; below, LOC.)

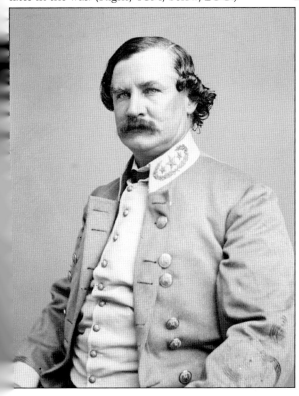

A native of Giles County, John Calvin Brown practiced law before secession. He served as colonel of the 3rd Tennessee Infantry at Fort Donelson and surrendered with the garrison. Later exchanged, he received promotions to brigadier and major general. He received a severe wound at Franklin and was given parole in North Carolina with the Army of Tennessee. After the war, he entered politics and eventually became the first Democratic governor following Reconstruction. He appears here in his Masonic garb. (TSLA.)

A native of Ohio and a graduate of the U.S. Military Academy, Bushrod Rust Johnson served in the Seminole and Mexican Wars before leaving the army to teach. Teaching at the University of Nashville when Tennessee seceded, Johnson commanded a Tennessee brigade in the Army of Tennessee until the winter of 1863, after which he served with the Army of Northern Virginia until the surrender at Appomattox. After the war, Johnson served as chancellor of the University of Nashville. (LOC.)

Born near Castalian Springs in Sumner County, William Brimage Bate served as a clerk on a steamboat, edited a newspaper, practiced law, worked in the state legislature, and participated in the Mexican War in the antebellum period. With the outbreak of the Civil War, he joined the 2nd Tennessee Infantry and rose to be the colonel. Bate served in every major engagement of the Army of Tennessee and lost three horses from beneath him at Chickamauga, which earned him praise from Pres. Jefferson Davis and a promotion to major general. After the surrender of the Army of Tennessee, Bate practiced law before becoming governor of Tennessee in 1882. Elected to the Senate in 1886, he represented Tennessee in Washington until his death in 1905. (Emily and Ronnie Townes.)

Cadmus Marcellus Wilcox grew up in Tipton County and graduated from the U.S. Military Academy in 1846. He served in the Mexican War as a member of the 7th U.S. Infantry and received a brevet for gallantry at Chapultepec. He resigned when Tennessee seceded and served with the Army of Northern Virginia. He was highly regarded throughout the country, and four former Union generals and four former Confederate generals served as his pallbearers in 1890. (LOC.)

Born in Nashville, John Adams graduated from the U.S. Military Academy and served in the 1st Dragoons in the Mexican War. Upon secession, he joined the Confederacy and rose from captain to brigadier general. He led his brigade into the assault at Franklin and fell mortally wounded attempting to jump his horse over the Union breastworks. His battle-riddled saddle survived and is in the Tennessee Historical Society Collection at the State Museum. (TSM.)

Although he is normally associated with Mississippi, William Barksdale was a native of Smyrna, Tennessee. He received his education at the University of Nashville and then moved to Columbus, Mississippi, to study law. A veteran of the Mexican War, Barksdale represented Mississippi in Congress until secession. He commanded a regiment and later a Mississippi brigade in the Army of Northern Virginia until his death at Gettysburg on July 3, 1863. (LOC.)

Tyree Harris Bell grew up in Sumner County, Tennessee. Early in the war, Bell commanded the 12th Tennessee Infantry at Belmont, Shiloh, and in Kentucky. In 1863, Bell transferred to Forrest's cavalry and commanded a brigade until the end of the war. He was one of Forrest's best commanders, but he did not receive his commission to brigadier general until 1865. After the war, Bell lived in California. He died en route home after a Confederate veterans reunion in 1902. (TSM.)

John Carpenter Carter moved to Lebanon, Tennessee, to attend Cumberland University. After graduation, he taught at Cumberland, married the daughter of one of the instructors, and eventually moved to Memphis. He started the war as a captain in the 38th Tennessee Infantry, later winning promotion to colonel. He eventually became brigadier general while serving with the Army of Tennessee. He received a mortal wound at Franklin and died 11 days later. Bishop Charles Quintard (page 115) presided over the funeral. (TSLA.)

Born near Pulaski, George Washington Gordon attended Western Military Institute and worked as a surveyor. He joined the 11th Tennessee Infantry and received his appointment as colonel in late 1862. He fought at Murfreesboro, Chickamauga, and Atlanta. He served as a brigadier general at Franklin and received a severe wound, spending the remainder of the war as a prisoner of war. He lived in Memphis after the war, served in Congress, and was a member of the Ku Klux Klan. (TSLA.)

A farmer from White County, George Gibbs Dibrell attended the Tennessee secession convention as a Unionist delegate. However, after Tennessee seceded, he enlisted in the 25th Tennessee Infantry Regiment and won election to lieutenant colonel. In the summer of 1862, he received authorization to raise the 8th Tennessee Cavalry Regiment and to serve as its colonel. The regiment fought initially with Forrest but later served in General Wheeler's cavalry command. Although not promoted to brigadier general until January 1865, Dibrell commanded a cavalry brigade for most of the war. He and his brigade surrendered in May 1865 in Washington, Georgia, while fulfilling their last assignment of guarding the archives of the Confederate government. Dibrell returned to White County after the war and served in the U.S. Congress. (Alabama Department of Archives and History.)

Robert Hatton began the war as colonel of the 7th Tennessee Infantry Regiment and led the unit to defend Virginia in 1861. Promoted to brigadier general in 1862, Hatton commanded the Tennessee Brigade, consisting of the 1st (Provisional), 7th, and 14th Tennessee Infantry Regiments. He received a mortal wound at the Battle of Seven Pines, Virginia, in May 1862. A monument to Hatton stands on the square in Lebanon, Tennessee. (LOC.)

Located in a photograph album containing several 7th Tennessee soldiers from Wilson County, this *carte-de-visite* (calling card) is an early-war image of Harry Thompson Hays as colonel of the 7th Louisiana Infantry. Hays was born in Wilson County and lived in Mississippi after his parents died. As an adult, he moved to New Orleans. A veteran of the Mexican War, Hays commanded the Louisiana Brigade in the Army of Northern Virginia for most of the war. (TSM.)

Born in Warren County, Benjamin Jefferson Hill worked as a merchant in McMinnville and served in the state senate. Hill gallantly commanded the 35th Tennessee Infantry until late 1863, when he received the appointment as provost marshal of the Army of Tennessee. In August 1864, he transferred to Forrest's cavalry command, where he remained until the end of the war. He returned to the mercantile business after the war and practiced law until his death in 1880. (Bruce Holher.)

George Maney, a native of Franklin, served in the Mexican War in the 1st Tennessee and in the 3rd Dragoons. He served in the Tennessee General Assembly from 1849 to 1851. During the Civil War, Maney rose from captain to brigadier general and commanded a brigade of Tennesseans until the fall of Atlanta. He worked for the railroads after the war and served in various diplomatic posts in South America. He died in 1901. (Emily and Ronnie Townes.)

Born in Henry County, William Hicks Jackson graduated from the U.S. Military Academy in 1856 and served with the Mounted Rifle Regiment until resigning in 1861. Initially he served in the artillery, but he soon commanded the 7th Tennessee Cavalry Regiment. Jackson earned promotion to brigadier general and commanded a brigade and later a division of cavalry attached to General Polk's Army of Mississippi. After the war, Jackson established Belle Meade Plantation in Nashville as the country's premier Thoroughbred racehorse center. (National Archives.)

Ben McCulloch's reputation as a fighter preceded the Civil War. Born in Rutherford County, he followed his friend David Crockett to Texas and fought at the Battle of San Jacinto in 1836. He remained in Texas and provided excellent service to Zachary Taylor as a Texas Ranger in the Mexican War. Commissioned a brigadier general in 1861, McCulloch achieved victory at the Battle of Wilson's Creek, Missouri. He died in combat at Elk Horn Tavern, Arkansas, in March 1862. (LOC.)

William Andrew Quarles practiced law in Clarksville and served as a judge, a railroad president, and an active member in Democratic politics. As colonel of the 42nd Tennessee, he spent time as a prisoner of war after the fall of Fort Donelson. He served in Mississippi and Louisiana after his promotion to brigadier general in 1863 and joined the Army of Tennessee for the Atlanta campaign. Wounded and captured at Franklin, he received his parole in 1865 and returned to law and state politics. (TSLA.)

Born near Mechanicsville, Thomas Benton Smith attended the Nashville Military Institute and worked for the railroad. He served as a lieutenant in Company B, 20th Tennessee, until elected colonel in May 1862. Promoted to brigadier general in July 1864, Smith commanded a brigade until captured at Nashville. After his surrender, Union colonel William McMillen of the 95th Ohio struck the unarmed Smith about the head with his saber. Smith suffered from brain damage and spent the remainder of his life in and out of the state asylum. (Emily and Ronnie Townes.)

Brig. Genl. O. F. Strahl
Cheatham's Division
Killed at Franklin Tenn. Hardee's Corps
Nov. 30th 1864. Army of T.

Otho French Strahl, a native of Ohio, relocated to Somerville, Tennessee, and practiced law with future Confederate general Daniel H. Reynolds. Living in Dyersburg at the war's outset, Strahl joined the 4th Tennessee Infantry and rose to the rank of colonel in January and to brigadier general in July 1863. He was noted for his gallantry at Chickamauga and commanded his brigade ably throughout the Atlanta campaign. Strahl died in the hand-to-hand fighting at Franklin on November 30, 1864. (TSLA.)

Virginian Alfred Jefferson Vaughan Jr. graduated from the Virginia Military Institute. Vaughan served as colonel of the 13th Tennessee Infantry and received promotion to brigadier general in November 1863. He lost a leg to an artillery burst near Atlanta in the summer of 1864. He survived his wound and lived in Memphis after the war. He served as the criminal court clerk of Shelby County and as commander of the Tennessee Division of the United Confederate Veterans. (LOC.)

John Crawford Vaughn openly supported secession in a region dominated by pro-Unionists. He witnessed the attack on Fort Sumter, participated at the Battle of First Manassas, and commanded a brigade at Vicksburg. Captured and exchanged, his brigade returned to East Tennessee and served as mounted infantry. In 1864 and 1865, his brigade fought in Virginia, Tennessee, and North Carolina and escorted Jefferson Davis in his flight from Richmond. Vaughn and his command surrendered in May 1865 near Washington, Georgia. (Thomasville, Georgia, Historical Society.)

John Wilkins Whitfield served as a captain in the 1st Tennessee and as lieutenant colonel of the 2nd Tennessee in the Mexican War. This Williamson County native moved to Missouri in the 1850s and worked as an Indian agent. At the outbreak of the Civil War, Whitfield lived in Kansas but commanded a Texas regiment. Commissioned brigadier general in May 1863, he commanded a brigade under William Hicks Jackson. He lived in Texas after the war and served in the legislature. (LOC.)

Born in Maury County and of Swiss decent, Felix Zollicoffer served as a printer and newspaper editor before being elected state printer of Tennessee in 1835. He saw military service in Florida as a lieutenant in the Second Seminole War. Upon his return, he edited the *Republican Banner*, the voice of the Whig Party. He was actively involved in state politics and served as state comptroller, adjutant general, and senator. In the election of 1860, he strongly supported fellow Tennessean John Bell, but upon secession, he accepted a commission as brigadier general and commanded the Department of East Tennessee. He worked diligently to keep peace in this volatile region. He moved his command into Kentucky in January 1862 and was attacked. Fought in a driving rainstorm, the Battle of Mill Springs, Kentucky, resulted in Zollicoffer's death. He was the first high-ranking Tennessean to die in battle. (Anthony Hodges.)

Three

CAVALIERS AND PARTISANS

Robert E. Lee described his cavalry under James Ewell Brown "J. E. B." Stuart as "the eyes and ears" of the Army of Northern Virginia. Lee's simple statement, although true, inadequately described the various roles the Confederate cavalry played in the Western theater. In reality, Confederate cavalry not only conducted reconnaissance, but they also delivered lighting-fast attacks to vulnerable supply lines, covered retreats, and in some instances served in the trenches alongside their infantry comrades.

Tennessee's cavalry regiments served exclusively with the armies of the Western theater, and members shed their blood in Kentucky, Tennessee, Mississippi, Alabama, Georgia, North and South Carolina, and Virginia, with some units having fought in Missouri, Indiana, and Ohio. Tennessee cavalrymen fought in every major campaign of the Western theater and participated in large battles and thousands of skirmishes due to their mobility.

The vast majority of Tennessee cavalry regiments served under the command of either Gen. Joe Wheeler or Nathan Bedford Forrest. Wheeler's cavalry normally operated in conjunction with the main army, while Forrest increasingly operated independently. Another independent commander, John Hunt Morgan, excelled in guerrilla warfare and often encouraged the creation of guerrilla or partisan units, which operated locally against supply lines or occupation troops. Several irregular units claimed that John Hunt Morgan commissioned their officers, though he did not have that authority.

Tennessee provided nearly 30 regiments of cavalry to the Confederate cause, as well as a number of smaller battalions and independent squadrons. Many of these units started as partisan ranger units but evolved into regular cavalry regiments. Due to the manner by which the Confederate War Department assigned regimental numbers, many Tennessee regiments adopted one number, only to have Richmond designate them as something different. Confusion resulted and remains. As an example, two different 4th Tennessee Cavalry Regiments fought at Chickamauga—one in Wheeler's Division and the other in Forrest's. For clarity, all regiments are identified by a regimental number followed by the name of the commander. Confederate officers used this method, and it retained in this text as well.

Written on this ambrotype of an unidentified Tennessee soldier was the following inscription: "A Tennessee volunteer, wounded and who (it is said) gallantly remarked, 'If I can't fight, I can still fiddle!' " This rare image of a Confederate soldier with a musical instrument shows the subject wearing a slouch hat, a double-breasted frock coat, and riding boots. (TSM.)

Thomas Claiborne of Nashville attended the U.S. Military Academy, graduating in the class of 1846. He joined the Mounted Rifle Regiment, served with distinction in the Mexican War, and remained in the army until secession. He joined the Confederate army and served as colonel of the 1st Confederate Cavalry Regiment, which consisted of companies from Kentucky and Tennessee. In the fall of 1863, Claiborne transferred from the regiment and served as a staff officer until the surrender. (TSM.)

Col. Frank N. McNairy

Killed in Second battle of Fort Donelson

Frank Nathaniel McNairy belonged to a prominent Nashville family. With the outbreak of the war, McNairy served as colonel of the 1st Tennessee Cavalry Battalion and fought at Mill Springs, Kentucky. In June 1862, the Confederate War Department consolidated the 1st and the 7th Battalions to form the 2nd Tennessee Cavalry Regiment (Barteau's). McNairy resigned after the consolidation and received permission to form his own partisan ranger unit. While in the process of recruiting, McNairy volunteered as a staff officer for Nathan Bedford Forrest. In the winter of 1863, Forrest's and Wheeler's cavalries attacked the Union garrison at Fort Donelson. The attack failed, and McNairy died in the fighting. (TSLA/THS.)

Alabama native Alex Key served in one of the elite units to participate in the Civil War. Created in 1862, Nathan Bedford Forrest's Escort Company served as scouts, bodyguards, and shock troops for their famous general. Forrest ensured that the company received the best firearms, and inspection returns indicate that each man carried a Sharps carbine. Key's photograph shows a Confederate carbine sling to support his carbine when mounted. (Anthony Hodges.)

The Adjutant and Inspector General Office in Richmond created the 1st Tennessee Cavalry (Wheeler's) in June 1862 by consolidating the 2nd and 11th Tennessee Battalions. William Stewart Hawkins began the war as second lieutenant of Company B, 11th Battalion, a unit composed of Davidson County men. With the consolidation, Hawkins served as major. He appeared for this photograph wearing the insignia of a Confederate colonel, although no record of his promotion survives. (Emily and Ronnie Townes.)

Asa Freeman served as the captain of Company F, the "Maury County Braves," 6th (Wheeler's) Tennessee Cavalry Regiment. Freeman, an uncle of the famous diarist Sam Watkins of the 1st Tennessee Infantry, loaned Sam a horse so that he could temporarily join the cavalry. Captain Freeman suffered severe wounds through both thighs while fighting along the Dallas–New Hope line north of Atlanta in May 1864. (TSM.)

William Leonidas Henderson joined Gantt's Battalion in 1861. When that unit surrendered at Fort Donelson, Private Henderson was at home sick with measles. Upon his recovery, he joined Company E, 1st Tennessee Cavalry (Wheeler's), and served until the surrender in North Carolina, having fought at Holly Springs, Mississippi; Thompson Station, Tennessee; and Chickamauga and New Hope Church, Georgia. He lived in Spring Hill after the war. (Bruce Holher.)

Henry M. Ashby raised a company in Knox County and won notoriety when they captured Unionists located near Cumberland Gap. Eventually his unit developed into the 2nd Tennessee. Ashby became colonel and commanded a brigade and a division in Wheeler's Cavalry. After the war, he settled near Atlanta, but he returned to Knoxville in 1868 to face an indictment. Ashby died from a gunshot wound in an altercation with the prosecuting attorney. (LOC.)

William T. Lane joined the 19th Tennessee Infantry when the war began but transferred to Company C, 16th Cavalry Battalion. Discharged for being too young, Lane reenlisted in his former unit when he was 18 years old. In the last two years of the war, Lane received wounds at Whitepost and Winchester, Virginia. He received a promotion to second lieutenant in September 1864 and ended the war as part of Jefferson Davis's escort. After the war, he returned to McMinn County and practiced law. (Anthony Hodges.)

The Reverend D. C. Kelley served in Forrest's 3rd Tennessee Cavalry. Kelley, a full-time Methodist minister, began the war as the second-in-command in Nathan Bedford Forrest's regiment. As Forrest rose to higher rank, Kelley was put in charge of "Forrest's old regiment" until the end of the war and was considered one of Forrest's most trusted leaders. He returned to the ministry after the war. (LOC.)

Pleasant A. Smith enlisted in Company A, 2nd Tennessee Cavalry (Barteau's). Smith served as the purchasing officer for Gen. Frank C. Armstrong. In October 1862, he returned to the 2nd to serve as adjutant. By the end of the war, Smith served as acting assistant inspector general for Gen. Tyree Bell. He returned to Nashville after the war and hosted two reunions at his home in 1885 and 1888. (TSM/THS.)

John M. Cantrell, born near Gallatin, received his education in local schools and moved to Florida in 1850. He returned to Sumner County in 1855 and joined Company D, Barteau's 2nd, at the outbreak of war. Commissioned second lieutenant in May 1864, Cantrell received a wound to the thigh at Harrisburg and lost his horse from beneath him near Florence, Alabama, in November 1864. After the war, he returned to farming and served six years as sheriff of Sumner County. (TSM/THS.)

George Edward Seay, a native of Hartsville, attended Cumberland University. He began the war as a member of the 2nd Tennessee Infantry but transferred to the cavalry and served as lieutenant in Company E, 2nd Tennessee Cavalry (Barteau's). Seay temporarily commanded the regiment at the battle of Harrisburg, Mississippi, when his superiors fell killed or wounded. During this battle, Seay's life was spared when bullets struck his canteen and pocket watch instead of him. Seay served as a chancery court judge after the war. (TSM/THS.)

J. Newsome Penuel, a native of Davidson County, relocated to Fountain Head, Sumner County, with his family in 1860 and engaged in farming. He enlisted in Company F, Barteau's 2nd Tennessee, in October 1861 and served as third lieutenant until captured in November 1863. For the remainder of the war, he was held at Camp Chase, Ohio. After the war, he worked as a guard at the state prison before going into the furniture business in Nashville. (TSM/THS.)

Jonathan M. Eastes served as captain of Company G, 2nd Tennessee Cavalry (Barteau's). The 2nd charged into a Union ambush at Harrisburg, Mississippi, on July 13, 1864, and Captain Eastes suffered a mortal wound in the first volley. Just after midnight, Colonel Barteau wrote his wife, "I lost thirty or more killed and wounded; six officers badly wounded. Lieutenant French and Captain Eastes, I think will die in a few hours." His comrades buried him near Verona, Mississippi. (TSM/THS.)

G. K. Crump enlisted in Company B, Barteau's 2nd Tennessee Cavalry, on November 1, 1863, at Okolona, Mississippi. Private Crump may be the same G. K. Crump who served with the 3rd Tennessee Infantry until deserting near Port Hudson, Louisiana, in 1863. The success and freewheeling actions of Forrest's cavalry often lured soldiers away from infantry units to join the cavalry. (TSM/THS.)

Buck H. Moore began the war as a private in Company E, 7th Cavalry Battalion, which eventually became Company G of Barteau's 2nd Tennessee Cavalry Regiment. He ultimately served as captain and had a horse shot from beneath him at Okolona, Mississippi. Wounded, he lost a second horse at Franklin, Tennessee, on November 30, 1864. He returned to his unit for the final campaigns of Forrest's cavalry in Alabama in 1865, only to have a third horse shot from beneath him. He survived the war and returned to New Middleton, Smith County, where he farmed and raised livestock. (Right, TSM/THS; below, TSM.)

F. M. McRee (or McRae), of Obion County, began the war as a member of the 9th Tennessee Infantry. Discharged for being underage, he returned home and assisted in raising Company F of Barteau's 2nd Tennessee Cavalry and eventually served as first lieutenant. The concussion of an artillery shell sent him to the hospital on July 13, 1864, near Harrisburg, Mississippi, but he returned to command two days later. During the battle of Brice's Crossroads, he commanded the company and succeeded in capturing a company of U.S. Colored Troops. During Hood's Tennessee campaign in 1864, the young lieutenant commanded the advance guard and was part of the rear guard during the retreat after the Battle of Nashville. Fighting a rearguard action at Hollow Tree Gap, McRee found himself cut off from his command and surrendered. A Union officer, described by the regimental historian for Barteau's 2nd Tennessee as a "drunken coward," shot McRee after his surrender. He survived the war and farmed by day and studied medicine by night. He graduated from Vanderbilt's medical school in 1879 and practiced medicine in Obion County. (TSM/THS.)

W. W. Hawkins served in Company C, 2nd Tennessee Cavalry (Barteau's), from the beginning of the war. Hawkins received a promotion to corporal in May 1862. Wounded at Okalona, Mississippi, in February 1864, he returned to the company only to be wounded again at Fort Pillow in April. The regimental historian, R. R. Hancock, knew Hawkins and speculated that his Fort Pillow wound led to his death after the war. (Daniel J. Taylor.)

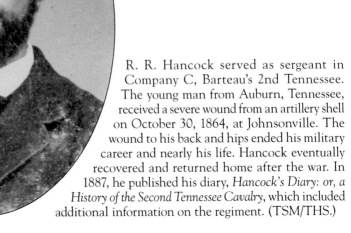

R. R. Hancock served as sergeant in Company C, Barteau's 2nd Tennessee. The young man from Auburn, Tennessee, received a severe wound from an artillery shell on October 30, 1864, at Johnsonville. The wound to his back and hips ended his military career and nearly his life. Hancock eventually recovered and returned home after the war. In 1887, he published his diary, *Hancock's Diary: or, a History of the Second Tennessee Cavalry*, which included additional information on the regiment. (TSM/THS.)

John D. McLin, of Auburn, Tennessee, served at various times as a courier, clerk, and first sergeant of Company C, Barteau's 2nd Tennessee. Wounded in a skirmish in Lewis County in 1864, McLin spent the rest of the war as a prisoner at Camp Douglas, Illinois. After the war, McLin served as the editor of the *Weekly American* newspaper, which was published in Nashville, and assisted in composing the regimental history. (TSM/THS.)

Edward S. Payne served in Company D, Barteau's 2nd. In the regimental photographic album assembled after the war, Payne is identified as living in Enon College, Tennessee. The 2nd Tennessee Cavalry served throughout the war with Nathan Bedford Forrest, and after the war, surviving members held yearly regimental reunions beginning in 1884. In 1885, they invited the survivors of Morton's Battery to join their veteran's organization. (TSM/THS.)

William Stalcup served in Company E of Colonel Barteau's 2nd Tennessee Cavalry Regiment. The regiment engaged with Union forces at Harrisburg, Mississippi, in July 1864 and fought for some time unsupported. Stalcup, like over 30 of his comrades, suffered from wounds received on July 14, 1864. He survived the war and attended the regiment's reunions. He appears here with his daughter Lethia. (TSM/THS.)

William T. "Billy" Nichols served throughout the war with Company G, Barteau's 2nd Tennessee Cavalry. During the siege of Nashville by the Army of Tennessee, Forrest's cavalry with a division of infantry moved to threaten Murfreesboro. Despite Forrest's best efforts, the expedition accomplished very little. Billy Nichols died from the wounds he received on December 7, 1864, at Murfreesboro. Lt. George Hager described Nichols as "the bravest of the brave." (TSM/THS.)

This rare tintype shows James M. Link after the war with his surveying equipment. Link enliste[d]
in Company F, Barteau's 2nd Tennessee Cavalry. Wounded in the shoulder at Fort Pillow in Apr[il]
1864, Link survived the war and worked as the Sumner County surveyor. He remained active i[n]
the regimental reunions until his death in 1926. (TSM/THS.)

Thomas Petway served throughout the war with Company G, Barteau's 2nd Tennessee Cavalry, and attended some of the reunions after the war. As Forrest's cavalry attempted to stop General Wilson's raid into Alabama in 1865, Petway received a gunshot wound on April 2 near Tuscaloosa, Alabama. (TSM/THS.)

David Reeves served as a private in Company G, Barteau's 2nd Tennessee Cavalry, and died in a small skirmish with the 1st Alabama Volunteer Cavalry (U.S.) in northern Mississippi on October 26, 1863. His comrades buried him in Fulton, Mississippi, the next day. (TSM/THS.)

Clabe (or Claib) West of Company G, Barteau's 2nd, received a severe wound at Harrisburg, Mississippi. West, William Forrest, and Allen Wythe entered the Gayso Hotel on horseback in search of Union officers during the Memphis raid in August 1864. When Forrest's command forced the steamboat *Mazzepa* to surrender near Johnsonville, Tennessee, in October 1864, West paddled across the Tennessee River to take possession of the ship. He lived in Carthage after the war. (TSM/THS.)

James Wellborn Starnes moved to Franklin, Tennessee, at a young age. As an adult, he practiced medicine, managed his agricultural pursuits in Tennessee and Mississippi, and served as an assistant surgeon with the 1st Tennessee in the Mexican War. With the outbreak of the Civil War, Dr. Starnes raised a cavalry company but soon commanded the 4th Tennessee (Starnes-McLemore's) and later a brigade under General Forrest. In an engagement in June 1863 near Tullahoma, Starnes received a mortal wound. (Emily and Ronnie Townes.)

Pvt. Samuel Alexander Owen(s) served in Company G, 4th Tennessee Cavalry Regiment (Starnes's). While his regiment was engaged in the defense of Atlanta, Union troops capture Owen near Lynnville in Giles County. The reason for his presence in an area so removed from his regiment is unclear. He spent six months at Camp Douglas as a prisoner. He took the oath of allegiance in December 1864 and thus secured his release. (TSLA.)

The reverse of this image bears the inscription, "R. Stewart, Company H, 4th Tennessee Cavalry, nineteen years old when was taken." There are two Robert Stewarts who served in different 4th Tennessee regiments. This image is most likely Robert Stewart. Union troops captured Robert Stewart in DeKalb County, Alabama, in March 1865. He spent the remainder of the war in the prison camp at Camp Chase, Ohio. (Anthony Hodges.)

Willis Scott Bledsoe practiced law in Fentress County and even represented Champ Ferguson in a murder trial before the war. Bledsoe recruited a company of partisans and operated along the Cumberland Plateau in conjunction with Confederate guerrilla chieftain Champ Ferguson for the first part of the war. Bledsoe's company later became part of the 4th Tennessee (Murray's), and Bledsoe served as the major. Fearful for reprisals from Unionists, Bledsoe moved to Cleburne, Texas, after the war. (Emily and Ronnie Townes.)

Although his name does not appear on any official muster rolls, William Jackson Blackwell joined Company A of the 5th Tennessee Cavalry (McKenzie's) in 1862 and remained with the unit throughout the war. His brother, J. L. Blackwell, served first as captain of Company A and later as the regiment's major. The regiment participated in the Battle of Chickamauga and all subsequent campaigns of the Army of Tennessee. William Blackwell returned to his home in Hamilton County after the war. (Anthony Hodges.)

John Newton Sligar enlisted in Company C, 5th Tennessee Cavalry (McKenzie's), at Decatur, Tennessee. During the fighting around Atlanta, Union troops took the young man prisoner at Ruff's Mill. Shipped to Camp Douglas, the McMinn County native's records reflect that he was "loyal [to the Union] and enlisted through false representation; he desires to take the oath of allegiance." (TSLA.)

John D. Huhn enlisted in Company C, 7th Tennessee Cavalry Regiment (Duckworth's), on June 6, 1861. Huhn served as third sergeant before his promotion to first sergeant in January 1864. He received multiple wounds to the head and arm at Brice's Crossroads in June 1864, and for his gallantry, a promotion to regimental adjutant soon followed. This photograph shows Huhn after his promotion to adjutant. He survived the war and returned to Memphis. (TSLA.)

Robert Ivey enlisted in the McDonald Dragoons in Memphis in 1861. This unit became Company A of Nathan Bedford Forrest's original regiment (3rd Tennessee Cavalry or 26th Cavalry Battalion). Ivey served as a corporal and sergeant in the company until his election as second lieutenant. He surrendered with the remnant of Forrest's command on May 11, 1865, in Gainesville, Alabama. (Emily and Ronnie Townes.)

Col. George Dibrell (page 31) formed a partisan ranger unit to operate along the Cumberland Plateau. The unit evolved into a full regiment known as the 8th Tennessee Cavalry (Dibrell's), which served under Generals Forrest and Wheeler. Jesse Barnes officially enlisted for the war in September 1862 in White County and served as a corporal. Obviously dressed for winter campaigning, Barnes appears in his overcoat and scarf. (Dr. Sam Barnes and the Cookeville Museum of History.)

John P. W. Brown wanted desperately to serve in the Confederate army. Only 15 years old when the war started, he escaped from Union-occupied Nashville after his 17th birthday and attempted to gain Confederate lines. Captured by Union troops, he and a comrade were confined in the state penitentiary. In October 1862, he managed to escape and finally joined Company G, 8th Tennessee Cavalry Regiment (Dibrell's). He resided in Nashville after the war and joined the Ku Klux Klan. (TSLA/Emily and Ronnie Townes.)

John "Jack" E. Rucker served as a corporal in Company B, 11th Tennessee Cavalry Regiment. Created in 1863 by the consolidation of Holman's and Douglas's Battalions, the regiment contained men from counties throughout Middle Tennessee. Rucker lived in Franklin, Williamson County, Tennessee, and surrendered with Forrest in Alabama at the end of the war. (Emily and Ronnie Townes.)

Company G of Biffle's 19th Tennessee Cavalry Regiment consisted of men from Maury County and counted G. H. "Hardy" Harbeson among its ranks. The regiment served at various times with Forrest and Wheeler and fought at Parker's Crossroads, Thompson Station, Chickamauga, McMinnville, the Atlanta campaign, and the Tennessee campaign. Captured at some point, Harbeson died in a prison camp. His brother Polk (page 82) also died in the war. (Bruce Holher.)

Samuel Farrow enlisted in the 21st Tennessee Cavalry Regiment (Wilson's) in May 1863. The regiment clashed with Union forces in Tennessee, Mississippi, and Alabama for the last years of the war under the leadership of General Forrest. Farrow appears in an overshirt and proudly displays the tool of his trade, a Colt Navy revolver. With the outcome of the war all but decided, Farrow went AWOL in March 1865. (Emily and Ronnie Townes.)

Tennessee's most notorious irregular warrior, Champ Ferguson, operated along the Upper Cumberland Plateau for most of the war and waged a brutal brand of guerrilla warfare against pro-Unionists. Occasionally, he also served as a scout for John Hunt Morgan, Joe Wheeler, and Willis Bledsoe. In 1864, Ferguson participated in the Battle of Saltville, Virginia. After the battle, Ferguson executed Union officers in the Confederate hospital at Emory and Henry College. At the end of the war, Ferguson and his command surrendered with the understanding that they would be treated as other Confederate troops. However, Union authorities arrested Ferguson several weeks later. Tried and convicted for war crimes, Champ Ferguson was hanged by Union authorities at the state penitentiary in October 1865. (*Frank Leslie's Illustrated Newspaper* in the collection of TSM.)

By 1863, Tennessee was gripped by chaotic guerrilla warfare. In response, Union commander adopted harsh measures to curtail spying and guerrilla actions. Meanwhile, the Confederate developed several scout units and encouraged the creation of irregular units. Coleman's Scout consisted predominately of Middle Tennessee soldiers detached from their original units for th special outfit. Sam Davis (left), a graduate of the Western Military Institute, and John Davi (right) of Rutherford County joined Coleman's Scouts. A Kansas unit captured Sam Davis i Giles County and discovered sensitive information on his person. In a drumhead trial, Unio officers convicted Davis of spying and sentenced him to execution. Offered a pardon if he wou divulge the source of his information, Davis replied, "I would rather die a thousand deaths tha to betray a friend or be false to duty." He was hanged in Pulaski, and his family recovered h remains and buried him at his home in Smyrna. The home of the "Boy Hero of the Confederacy is a state historic site. (Sam Davis Home Memorial Association.)

Benjamin Franklin Sheppard began the war as a member of the 4th Louisiana Infantry Battalion. Discharged in 1861, Sheppard returned home and joined another unit. Captured by Union troops and transported north, he escaped when Confederate troops derailed the train in Sumner County. He served the remainder of the war with Capt. Ellis Harper's Independent Scout Company, which attacked Union outposts and rail lines in Sumner, Wilson, Trousdale, and Robertson Counties. Sheppard never returned to Louisiana; he married and settled in Trousdale County. (Author's collection.)

Alexander Duval McNairy joined Company C, the "Sewanee Rifles," 20th Tennessee, in 1861 and briefly served as lieutenant. This image of McNairy shows him before his promotion and illustrates the uniforms unique to Company C. The regiment reorganized after the battle of Shiloh, and McNairy lost reelection. He returned to Tennessee and formed a partisan ranger unit that operated in Dickson, Cheatham, Hickman, Wayne, and Perry Counties. (TSLA.)

Isaac Bell was the youngest son of Gen. Tyree Bell (page 29) and served as a volunteer staff officer for his father for most of the war. General Bell's staff was not only his military family, it was also his real family; at least seven of his staff were related to him. Isaac survived the war and attempted to reestablish the family farm. He eventually moved to California with his father. (TSM.)

William Montgomery Forrest was the son of Gen. Nathan Bedford Forrest and followed his father to war at 15 in 1861. Commissioned a lieutenant in 1864, he served as an aide-de-camp on the general's staff. "Willie" befriended Samuel Donelson (page 110), who also served on the staff in the last year of the war. Wounded at Dover, Spring Hill, and Harrisburg, William survived the war and returned to Memphis. He died of a stroke in 1908. (TSM.)

Four

THE HARD MARCHING, HARD FIGHTING INFANTRY

The backbone of Civil War armies was the infantry soldier. While cavalry had the ability to raid and move rapidly, at the end of day, it was the infantry that spearheaded assaults, manned the trenches, and ultimately decided the outcome of Civil War battles. The infantry soldier, burdened with his rifle, accoutrements, rations, and knapsack, often marched 20 or more miles a day and endured constant exposure to the weather, all the while living on the scantiest of rations. The men who survived the daily routine and the horrors of Civil War battlefields were among the toughest soldiers in American history.

Tennessee provided over 60 regiments of infantry to the Confederacy. The vast majority of these regiments served in the Army of Tennessee or the Army of Mississippi, the principal armies tasked with defending Tennessee, Georgia, Alabama, Mississippi, and portions of Louisiana. By the end of the war, these hard-luck armies fought in Missouri, Kentucky, North Carolina, and South Carolina in addition to the five previously listed states. These soldiers experienced combat at Fort Donelson, Shiloh, Murfreesboro, Vicksburg, Chickamauga, Atlanta, Franklin, and Nashville. Most of the Tennessee soldiers surrendered two weeks after Appomattox, near Raleigh, North Carolina, on April 26, 1865.

While the majority of Tennessee infantry regiments served with the Western theater armies, a few regiments joined the Army of Northern Virginia and experienced combat around Richmond, at Sharpsburg, Fredericksburg, Gettysburg, and the Wilderness, and all of the battles of General Lee's army. Indeed, the 1st (Turney's), 7th, and 14th Tennessee Regiments spent the whole war in the east, and Tennessee general Robert Hatton commanded the brigade until his death at Seven Pines. Other Tennessee regiments joined James Longstreet's corps after the battle of Chickamauga and moved through East Tennessee to become part of the Army of Northern Virginia, where they remained until the surrender at Appomattox on April 9, 1865.

Thanks to the reminiscences of Sam Watkins, entitled *Company Aytch*, the 1st Tennessee remains one of the most famous regiments of the Civil War. Hume Feild served as the colonel for most of the war. Feild was one of the few officers to carry a rifle into battle and put his repeating rifle (probably a Henry) to use on many battlefields. He received a serious wound to the head at Kennesaw Mountain, Georgia, in June 1864, which left him paralyzed on one side. (Emily and Ronnie Townes.)

John F. Wheless commanded Company C of Feild's 1st Tennessee. Wheless became captain in May 1862. Fiercely engaged at Perryville in October 1862, the 1st lost over half of its command killed, captured, or wounded. Captain Wheless was one of the wounded and captured. Upon his return to the army, his health prevented him from commanding the company. He served on staff duty for General Polk until he resigned in March 1864. He then served as a paymaster in the Confederate Navy. (Emily and Ronnie Townes.)

Carey A. Harris served as second lieutenant in Company D, "The Williamson Grays," of Feild's 1st Tennessee Infantry. Harris spent most of the first year of the war at home sick. His absence from the regiment ensured that he did not win reelection when the regiment reorganized in May 1862. (Emily and Ronnie Townes.)

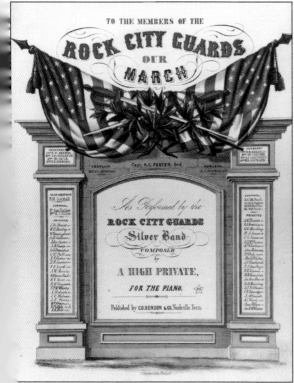

Created before the war, the Rock City Guards was a militia unit in Nashville. With the outbreak of the war, the Rock City Guards became Companies A, B, and C of Colonel Feild's 1st Tennessee Infantry Regiment. This image shows a sheet music cover for a song created for the Rock City Guards and performed by the battalion's band. (TSM.)

J. Clay March was a member of Company A, the Rock City Guards. March appears in a simple overshirt and has a Colt revolver suspended from his leather waist belt. March was wounded at the Battle of Murfreesboro and transferred to the engineers in May 1863. (Emily and Ronnie Townes and Daniel J. Taylor.)

Pvt. Robert A. Cheatham of Company C, 1st Tennessee (Feild's), proudly displays his company letter on his forage cap. Cheatham, only 17 at enlistment, served as an orderly to Gen. Samuel Donelson early in the war. He surrendered in Charlotte, North Carolina, in May 1865. (TSLA.)

Civil War battlefields left more men wounded than killed. George S. Nichol joined Company D, 1st Tennessee (Feild's), and spent most of 1862 in the hospital or detailed as a nurse. Nichol later joined Company F, 18th Tennessee Cavalry (Newsom's). In June 1864, he received a shotgun blast to the face, which damaged his left eye. The right image shows Nichol in his uniform; the image below shows him in civilian clothing. The damage to his eye is apparent. (Both, TSLA.)

Henry H. Cook began the war in Company D, 1st Tennessee (Feild's). He later became a lieutenant in the 44th Infantry (consolidated). The 44th fought at Drewry's Bluff, Virginia, in 1864, and Cook ended up a prisoner. In response to Andersonville, Union authorities moved Confederate prisoners to the coasts of Georgia and South Carolina as human shields, while also starving the 600 men, including Cook. He survived and wrote articles for *Confederate Veteran* detailing the experiences of the "Immortal Six Hundred." (TSLA.)

This ambrotype shows the three Brandon brothers of Maury County and members of Company H, 1st Tennessee (Feild's). Alexander William Brandon (left) was wounded at Perryville and spent much of 1863 detailed as a nurse in various hospitals. Edmond Brandon (center) survived the war only to be killed in Texas in 1869. James Maginnis Brandon (right), also wounded at Perryville, died on June 27, 1864, at the Battle of Kennesaw Mountain, Georgia. (Kennesaw Mountain National Military Park, Philip Bonine Collection.)

Some infantry units had regimental bands. Pvt. Junius Tucker of Company H, 1st Tennessee (Feild's), posed for his photograph wearing a frock coat, forage cap, and musician's sword and toting a saxhorn. Tucker's service records list him as the bugler of Company H and later as the chief musician of the 1st Tennessee. He also appears in the photograph below. Tucker (left) poses with an unidentified member of Company H, and both men wear forage caps. The top of Tucker's hat has brass letters that spell out "H / BAND / 1st / TENN." On the top of his comrade's cap is "Co. H / 1st / TENN." Having witnessed the carnage at Franklin, Tucker deserted to Union lines on December 11, 1864. He took the oath of allegiance on January 10, 1865. (Both, Emily and Ronnie Townes.)

Cpl. William Graham (left) and Joseph W. Bynum (right) belonged to Company H, 1st Tennessee (Feild's). The 1st served briefly in Virginia early in the war, and Joseph Bynum died before the regiment returned to Tennessee in 1862. Graham bravely crawled in front of the entrenchments at Kennesaw Mountain to place chevaux-de-frise, which were obstacles with spikes that were used to prevent attacks, and returned with prisoners. Graham would die within a week. He died in the fighting at Mount Zion Church, Georgia, on July 4, 1864. (Kennesaw Mountain National Military Park.)

James William Sarver, a member of the Fairfield community in Sumner County, enlisted in Company K of Col. William B. Bates's (page 27) 2nd Tennessee Infantry. In two days of heavy fighting at Shiloh in April 1862, the regiment lost nearly two-thirds of those engaged. Counted among those mortally wounded was the 20-year-old Sarver, who died on May 21, 1862, in a Confederate hospital in Columbus, Mississippi. (Courtesy of Patrick T. Meguiar.)

David B. Staley joined Company K, 2nd Tennessee (Robinson's), at Castalian Springs in May 1861. The captain of Company K was Humphrey Bate, brother of Gen. William Bate (page 27). Staley received a furlough on February 14, 1862, and presumably returned to Sumner County. Within a week, sections of Middle Tennessee were within Union lines due to the defeat at Fort Donelson. Staley's records indicate his absence "within enemy lines," and he never returned to his regiment. (Daniel J. Taylor.)

William M. Shuler, of Giles County, soldiered in Company D of John C. Brown's 3rd Tennessee Infantry (page 26). The 3rd Tennessee trained at Camp Cheatham in Robertson County before reporting to Fort Donelson. As Union troops encircled the fort in February 1862, the Confederates attempted a breakout. William Shuler died in the Confederate attack on February 15. Although the attack opened an escape route, inept Confederate leaders ordered them back to the trenches and surrendered Fort Donelson the next day. (Robert L. Parker.)

Another soldier to witness the Fort Donelson fiasco was James Giddens of Company C, 3rd Tennessee (Brown's). Giddens began the war as a sergeant but won election to junior second lieutenant in September 1861. Giddens survived the fighting at Fort Donelson and imprisonment at Johnson's Island. Exchanged at Vicksburg in September 1862, Giddens failed to win reelection and he no longer appeared on the rolls. The regiment fought in Mississippi and Louisiana before joining the Army of Tennessee before Chickamauga. (Emily and Ronnie Townes.)

Joseph L. Lett joined Company F, 4th Tennessee Infantry, in May 1861 and became the captain. The 4th Tennessee, commanded by Col. Otho F. Strahl (page 36), lost nearly half of those engaged at Shiloh and at Perryville. This forced the regiment to consolidate with the 5th Tennessee in December 1862. The consolidation forced Lett from his command, and he worked in the Conscription Bureau for General Pillow (page 20) until he received a medical discharge in November 1863. (Daniel J. Taylor.)

The Battle of Franklin, Tennessee, on November 30, 1864, essentially destroyed the Army of Tennessee. Thomas L. Murrell of Company H, 6th Tennessee Infantry, died with his army that day. Murrell enlisted at age 18 in Jackson, Tennessee. Union troops captured Murrell, furloughed for sickness, in May 1862 near Jackson. He returned to his unit in 1863 and received a severe wound at Chickamauga. He recovered, received a promotion to sergeant in 1864, but died in the carnage at Franklin. (TSM.)

The 7th Tennessee Infantry organized in Sumner County in 1861 but soon deployed to Virginia and remained with the Army of Northern Virginia until the surrender. When Col. Robert Hatton (page 32) rose to brigade command, John Fite Goodner of DeKalb County became colonel of the 7th. Artillery fire that killed General Hatton at Seven Pines also wounded Colonel Goodner. Plagued by his wounds, he resigned in April 1863. His wounds never healed, and he died in 1870. (TSM.)

Heavily engaged in the fighting in Virginia, Maryland, and Pennsylvania, the 7th Tennessee desperately needed replacement soldiers. James "Jess" Fairchild, a 44-year-old conscript from Hancock County, joined Company D in March 1864. Fairchild's involvement with the regiment was short-lived. He died in Richmond's Chimbrarazo Hospital on June 21, 1864. (TSM.)

John C. Hale (right) and his brother Thomas R. "Tammy" Hale (below) joined Company K, 7th Tennessee Infantry, in June 1861. Thomas died of disease at Healing Springs, Virginia, in October 1861. John transferred to Company B in May 1862 and suffered a head wound at Chancellorsville a year later. In the summer of 1863, he reported to a Richmond hospital with gonorrhea, but he returned to his regiment in August 1863. He died in the Wilderness fighting on May 5, 1864. (Right, TSM; below, Emily and Ronnie Townes.)

Archibald D. Norris enlisted as a private in Company K, 7th Tennessee Infantry, in May 1861 and soon won election to captain. The 7th Tennessee, as part of Heth's Division, temporarily pierced the Union line in the Pickett-Pettigrew charge at Gettysburg. Norris grabbed the regimental flag and wrapped it around his body to prevent its capture. Union troops took Norris prisoner on April 4, 1865. Held at Johnson's Island, Norris took the oath of allegiance on June 19, 1865. (Emily and Ronnie Townes.)

The 9th Tennessee Infantry consisted of men from West Tennessee. The regiment fought with the Army of Tennessee for the entirety of the war. Robert Marshall of Tipton County left his studies at Erskine College, South Carolina, and returned home to enlist in Company C. The 9th suffered heavy casualties at Perryville, Kentucky, in October 1862. Robert Marshall died in the fighting. (Tipton County Museum and Veterans Memorial Park.)

Having designed 40 buildings, Adolphus Heiman was one of the most popular antebellum architects in Nashville. A Prussian by birth, he moved to Nashville by 1841 and served in the Mexican War. Heiman served as the colonel of the 10th Tennessee and commanded a brigade at Fort Donelson. Surrendered with the garrison, he returned to the regiment after his exchange but died in Jackson, Mississippi, in July 1862. He appears here in his Mexican War uniform. (TSLA/THS.)

Randall McGavock, a former mayor of Nashville, actively courted the Irish vote throughout his political career. With the outbreak of war, McGavock and Adolphus Heiman raised the 10th Tennessee Infantry with a cadre of Irish Americans from Nashville, Clarksville, McEwen, and Giles County. After Heiman's death, McGavock commanded the regiment until his own death at the battle of Raymond, Mississippi, in May 1863. (TSLA.)

Capt. Samuel P. Kirkman commanded Company E, 10th Tennessee. While the regiment encamped at Fort Donelson in February 1862, the wife of Pvt. James McLauflin, of Company I, visited the camps and went into labor. Kirkman assisted in the birth of the child. Unfortunately, the child's father died of disease in Mississippi in 1862. Kirkman received a minor wound at Raymond and was taken prisoner on September 2, 1864, in Atlanta. He remained a captive at Johnson's Island until June 1865. (TSM/THS.)

Polk Harbeson served as a second lieutenant in Company I, 10th Tennessee Infantry. The company consisted of men from Clarksville and the surrounding countryside. There are few records related to Harbeson's service, but he apparently went to Johnson's Island after Fort Donelson and returned to the regiment in Mississippi after exchange. (Bruce Holher.)

Edward Pearl enlisted in Company D, the "Hermitage Guards," 11th Tennessee Infantry Regiment, at Nashville in May 1861. Pearl's records indicate that he deserted the regiment during the evacuation of Cumberland Gap in 1862. (Emily and Ronnie Townes.)

More Civil War soldiers died of diarrhea and dysentery than from combat, and Pvt. Sanford G. M. Jackson is an example. Sanford enlisted in Company K, 11th Tennessee Infantry, at Lenoir's Station in November 1862. Jackson died of chronic diarrhea in Oliver Hospital, located in Dalton, Georgia, on August 30, 1863. (Emily and Ronnie Townes.)

Albert Gallatin Harris operated a store and served as postmaster in Newbern, Tennessee. A cousin to Tyree Bell (page 29), Harris was the first lieutenant in Company A, 12th Tennessee, and Bell was the colonel. With the consolidation of the 12th and the 47th Tennessee in 1862, Bell became a supernumerary but raised a cavalry regiment. Bell later commanded a cavalry brigade, and Albert Harris, now a major, was his adjutant general. He survived the war and was a business partner with Bell. (Bruce Holher/Daniel J. Taylor.)

Joseph L. Granbery grew up in Macon, Fayette County, and graduated from the University of North Carolina in 1859. Governor Harris commissioned him as captain of the "Macon Grays," which became Company B, 13th Tennessee Infantry, under Col. Alfred J. Vaughn (page 36). Wounded at Shiloh, Granbery resigned his commission and joined the 12th Tennessee Cavalry. He appears here in the uniform of the Macon Grays. (TSM.)

Caleb B. Jones served as captain of Company L, the "Zollicoffer Avengers," 13th Tennessee Infantry, which was the last company to join the regiment on April 28, 1862. Company L missed the Battles of Belmont and Shiloh but marched into Kentucky in the fall of 1862. At the battle of Murfreesboro, the regiment was heavily engaged, and Captain Jones received a serious wound on December 31, 1862. He resigned his commission on April 24, 1863, and returned to Hardeman County. (Bruce Holher.)

T. M. Cartwright mustered in with Company B, 13th Tennessee, at Jackson on May 28, 1861. This 24-year-old Fayette County soldier was rarely absent from his regiment and received a promotion to corporal on January 1, 1864. He survived the war and lived in the Oakdale community. (Emily and Ronnie Townes.)

The 14th Tennessee Infantry served alongside the 1st (Turney's) and the 7th in the Army of Northern Virginia and witnessed all of the battles of General Lee's army. Joseph J. Neblett enrolled in Company H, 14th Tennessee, at Clarksville in May 1861. This 22-year-old Montgomery County farmer's career as a soldier was short-lived. He received a medical discharge for disability on January 1, 1862. (Emily and Ronnie Townes.)

John Savage, former lieutenant colonel of the 14th U.S. Infantry Regiment in the Mexican War, practiced law and served in Congress before the war. Savage commanded the 16th Tennessee in the Cheat Mountain Campaign (Virginia) and through the Battles of Perryville and Murfreesboro, in which the regiment suffered astonishingly high casualties. Passed over for promotion, Savage resigned his commission in 1863 and made an unsuccessful bid for governor. He lived in McMinnville after the war and served in the General Assembly. (LOC.)

The 17th Tennessee Infantry Regiment began the war in the Army of Tennessee and fought from Fishing Creek, Kentucky, through Longstreet's campaign in East Tennessee. Transferred to the Army of Northern Virginia with Longstreet in early 1864, the regiment fought in the defenses around Petersburg and Richmond and surrendered at Appomattox. Pvt. E. R. Dryden, of Company H, apparently witnessed all of the action. His records show him "present" at every roll call. (Emily and Ronnie Townes.)

William W. Kimbro joined Company C, 18th Tennessee, in Murfreesboro on August 7, 1861. The 26-year-old Rutherford County soldier served with his regiment at Fort Donelson and was part of the surrendered force. Sent to Camp Butler, Illinois, Kimbro died in captivity on May 14, 1862. (TSM.)

Three Carter brothers from Williamson County joined the 20th Tennessee in 1861, and their home would be the center point of the Battle of Franklin in November 1864. Moscow B. Carter served as lieutenant colonel of the regiment until captured at Mill Springs, Kentucky. Held as a prisoner of war, Moscow returned home on parole and took the oath of allegiance. While the fighting raged around his house, Moscow sheltered the Carter women, children, and slaves in the basement. (Battle of Franklin Trust.)

Capt. Theodoric "Todd" Carter joined his brothers in Company H, 20th Tennessee, in 1861. Promoted to captain and assistant quartermaster, Todd penned letters for Confederate newspapers under the alias "Mint Julep." As the Confederate army neared Franklin on November 30, 1864, Todd exclaimed, "Boys, I am going home." In the horrific charge, he fell mortally wounded in his family's garden. His brother Moscow recovered the young soldier, and he died in the house in which he had born. (Battle of Franklin Trust.)

Francis (Frank or Wad) Carter also served in Company H, 20th Tennessee. Wad served in the color guard until wounded at Shiloh. He received a medical discharge in August 1862. He moved to Texas and may have served in a Texas unit late in the war. (Battle of Franklin Trust.)

Another member of Company H was William Shy. Shy served as a lieutenant in Company H and ultimately served as captain. Upon the resignation of Col. Joel Battle and the promotion of Col. Thomas Benton Smith (page 35), Shy became colonel of the 20th Tennessee. During the Battle of Nashville, Union troops overran the hillside entrenchments held by the regiment. Shy refused to surrender and fell mortally wounded. The hill where Shy died now bears his name. (Anthony Hodges/Ronnie Mangrum.)

Patrick Duffy, an Irishman, served as the original captain of Company K, 20th Tennessee, but later served as regimental major and served as such at Shiloh. When the regiment reorganized and reenlisted for the duration of the war in the summer of 1862, Duffy failed to win reelection. Duffy hated to have his picture taken. This image of him was taken without his knowledge at one of the regiment's reunions after the war. (Anthony Hodges.)

In the summer of 1863, the Union army attempted to maneuver the Confederates out of Middle Tennessee. In June 1863, a Union brigade armed with Spencer repeating rifles charged toward Hoover's Gap, near Bell Buckle, Tennessee. General Bate's brigade, including the 20th Tennessee attempted to hold the gap but to no avail. Maj. Fred Claybrooke of Williamson County died in the fighting while commanding the regiment. (TSLA.)

The original colonel of the 20th Tennessee was Joel Battle of Nashville. His son Joel A. Battle Jr., pictured here, served as the regimental adjutant. Wounded at Fishing Creek, Kentucky, in January 1862, Joel returned to the regiment in time to fight at Shiloh in April. He died on the second day of the battle, and his father became a prisoner of war. (TSLA.)

William G. Ewin, from Davidson County, served initially as a lieutenant in Company A, the "Hickory Guards," 20th Tennessee. Promoted to captain in June 1862, Ewin served with the regiment and received a gunshot wound to the hip at Chickamauga from which he recovered. During the campaign for Atlanta, Ewin received a severe wound on June 22, 1864, which required the amputation of a leg. He spent the remainder of the war in army hospitals. (Emily and Ronnie Townes.)

The war divided many families, like the Peyton family of Sumner County. Bailey Peyton Sr. was active in politics and won accolades for his service at the Battle of Monterey in the Mexican War. He remained a strong Unionist with Tennessee's secession. His son Bailey Peyton Jr., pictured here, supported secession and was the first lieutenant of Company A, 20th Tennessee. Peyton Jr. died at the battle of Mill Spring, Kentucky, in January 1862, along with his father's friend, Gen. Felix Zollicoffer (page 38). (TSM.)

James Rawley (left) enlisted in Company C, the Sewanee Rifles, 20th Tennessee Regiment, in May 1861 and received a promotion to first lieutenant a year later. During the Atlanta campaign, Rawley received a severe wound to his leg at the Battle of Resaca on May 14, 1864. He apparently never returned to the regiment after his wounding. The other soldier is unidentified. (Daniel J. Taylor.)

Life as a prisoner of war during the Civil War was particularly harrowing. Confederates held in Northern prisons suffered in the harsh winters, received scant rations, and of course grappled with the mental issues of captivity. This image reportedly shows the members of Company H, 20th Tennessee, captured at Missionary Ridge in November 1863. It is possible, however, that this image dates to earlier in the war, perhaps showing the company members captured at Mill Springs in 1862. (Battle of Franklin Trust.)

James M. Harrison, of Williamson County, joined Company H, 20th Tennessee, and served alongside the Carter brothers (pages 88 and 89). Harrison spent much of 1863 sick, thus missing the Tullahoma campaign and the Battle of Chickamauga. Harrison deserted the regiment on February 23, 1864, and took the oath of allegiance three days later. (Battle of Franklin Trust.)

This rare image of a Confederate drummer shows W. G. Bryant, the musician of Company I, the Hermitage Guards. Bryant posed with his drum and wore a kepi and frock coat. Bryant lost the use of an arm at Shiloh in April 1862, which resulted in his discharge from the army on October 10, 1862. (Emily and Ronnie Townes.)

The 23rd Tennessee Infantry Regiment consisted of companies drawn from across Middle Tennessee. William Crisp Blanton served as the captain of Company F, which included men from Bedford and Marshall Counties. The regiment suffered heavy casualties at Shiloh, which forced its consolidation with the 17th Tennessee. Captain Blanton resigned his commission around the time of the consolidation. The regiment served with the Army of Tennessee and moved with Gen. James Longstreet into East Tennessee. The unit remained with the Army of Northern Virginia until Appomattox. (TSLA.)

William Crisp Blanton

The 24th Tennessee served with the Army of Tennessee for the entirety of the war. Company B of the 24th Tennessee contained men from Williamson County, and Henry J. Walker enlisted in Nolensville in August 1861. The regiment experienced its first combat at Shiloh on April 6, 1862. Killed in action that day was 20-year-old Pvt. Henry Walker. Walker's uniform jacket survives at the Carter House State Historic Site in Franklin, Tennessee. (Battle of Franklin Trust.)

Samuel W. Daimwood served in Company G, the "Duck River Rifles," of the 24th Tennessee Infantry Regiment. Daimwood was wounded at Shiloh but recovered to serve with the Army of Tennessee until the end of the war. He surrendered with the Army of Tennessee on April 26, 1865, at Greensboro, North Carolina. (TSLA.)

Elijah Anderson of Company K, 24th Tennessee Infantry, was also a casualty of the fighting at Shiloh. Anderson never recovered from his wounds and died several weeks later in a Confederate hospital in Corinth, Mississippi. (TSLA.)

Benjamin Dudley Franklin, of Sumner County, served in Company F, 30th Tennessee Infantry, as fourth sergeant. The 30th reported to Fort Donelson on November 27, 1861, and immediately went to work constructing buildings for the garrison, as well as digging entrenchments and gun emplacements. The labor and the weather contributed to the illness that struck Sergeant Franklin, and he was furloughed home sick. Franklin died at home on January 15, 1862, having never fired a shot at the Union army. (Ken Thomsen.)

J. P. McClain joined Company K, 31st Tennessee Infantry, at Trenton, Tennessee, in September 1861. The companies within this regiment all hailed from West Tennessee. McClain received a promotion to second lieutenant in August 1862 and moved with his regiment into Kentucky with the rest of the Army of Tennessee. McClain received a gunshot wound at Perryville. He died on October 15, 1863, in a Confederate hospital that had fallen into Union hands. (Emily and Ronnie Townes.)

The 34th Tennessee Infantry Regiment was odd in its composition in that the companies contained men from across Tennessee, as well as from Alabama and Mississippi. William Churchwell served as the colonel of the regiment and also as the garrison commander at Cumberland Gap. Churchwell later served as the provost marshal of Knoxville and attempted to counteract guerrilla warfare undertaken by the area's Unionists. (TSM.)

A member of Churchwell's regiment was Lymon C. Gunn of Nashville. Gunn served in Company F, the "Acklen Rifles," 34th Tennessee, until discharged in December 1861 due to typhoid fever contracted at Cumberland Gap. The 16-year-old escaped Nashville during Union occupation and volunteered as an aid to Gen. Simon Bolivar Buckner at Perryville. Even though he had applied to be a cadet in the Confederate army, he ended the war as a private attached to headquarters in the Department of Alabama. (Anthony Hodges.)

The 37th Tennessee consisted of companies from East and Middle Tennessee and one company from Alabama. Early in its formation, it was referred to as the 1st East Tennessee Rifles. The 28-year-old William Blackburn served as first lieutenant of Company B, which consisted of men from Claiborne County. Blackburn commanded the company for a time and also served as the regimental quartermaster. Inexplicably, Blackburn dropped from the regimental muster rolls in May 1862. (Daniel J. Taylor.)

S. M. Alexander enlisted at Dalton, Georgia, in Company A of the 41st Tennessee in April 1864, just before the Atlanta campaign began. Wounded at the Battle of Atlanta on July 22, 1864, Alexander spent the remainder of the war in hospitals in Mississippi. He received a furlough in March 1865 and received a parole when the Department of Alabama, Mississippi, and Louisiana surrendered in May 1865. Alexander listed his home as Lincoln County, Mississippi, and Talladega, Alabama. Alexander appears with a rare Bacon pistol. (Emily and Ronnie Townes.)

The 44th Tennessee consolidated with the 55th to form the 44th Consolidated Tennessee Infantry in April 1862. After the consolidation, Henry C. Ewin, formerly of the 55th Infantry Regiment, became the major. Mortally wounded at the battle of Murfreesboro on December 31, 1862, Ewin died at Westview plantation in Triune. (TSM.)

Lafayette W. Bush enlisted in Company G, 44th Tennessee, in Nashville on December 30, 1861. Bush spent most of his military career detailed as a nurse to the Confederate hospital at Catoosa Springs, Georgia, due to a weak eye. After his regiment joined the Army of Northern Virginia in early 1864, Bush returned to the infantry ranks. He died on September 29, 1864, when Union troops attacked Signal Hill, Virginia. (TSLA.)

DeWitt Smith, pictured here, served in the 45th Tennessee until he deserted to avenge the murder of his cousin Dee Jobe. Jobe served in Coleman's Scouts when captured near Triune in August 1864. He refused to reveal his mission, and his captors gouged out his eyes and cut out his tongue before they dragged him behind a horse. DeWitt Smith murdered no less than 50 Union soldiers in retaliation. Cornered near Nolensville, Smith died from his wounds before he could be executed. (Anthony Hodges.)

Tennessee had two 48th Tennessee regiments. When the majority of the 48th (Voorhie's) surrendered at Fort Donelson, those men not at Fort Donelson combined with remnants of other companies to form Nixon's 48th Tennessee. Eventually, both regiments consolidated. Henry Evans commanded the consolidated regiment in the summer of 1864. He is often listed as colonel, but he never received that promotion. (TSM.)

William Polk, the son of Lucius Polk and a nephew of Gen. Leonidas Polk (page 22), volunteered for the 3rd Tennessee Infantry Regiment when the war began. The Maury County native received a severe wound at Fort Donelson. He recovered and went on to serve as the adjutant of the 48th Tennessee Infantry (Voorhie's). After the war, he farmed in Mississippi until his death in 1906. (Emily and Ronnie Townes.)

Robertson Yeatman Johnson, a Montgomery County native, enrolled as third lieutenant in Company F, 49th Tennessee, in December 1861. As part of the Fort Donelson garrison, Johnson remained in Union prison camps until exchanged at Vicksburg in September 1862, after which he won election to captain. He survived the war and died in Montgomery County in 1908. (Emily and Ronnie Townes.)

The men of the 49th, along with the rest of the Army of Tennessee, moved toward Tennessee after the fall of Atlanta. Union and Confederate forces clashed at Franklin on November 30, 1864. The battle decimated the 49th. The following three soldiers were included among those captured: (from left to right) Charley Bailey, Eddie Read, and Charley Shanklin. A photographer took their photograph at Camp Douglas prison camp in Illinois after the battle. (Bruce Holher.)

Landon Cooper of Company A, 49th Tennessee Infantry Regiment, managed to escape from Fort Donelson before the surrender and made his way to Clarksville. He rejoined his regiment after their exchange in Mississippi. Cooper spent the rest of the war on detached duty as a hospital steward in Mobile, Alabama. He died in 1904, and his grave is on the grounds of the Hermitage, the home of Andrew Jackson. (Anthony Hodges.)

Company F, 50th Tennessee Infantry Regiment, contained men from Stewart County, and their mustering ground was Fort Donelson. The 18-year-old Jeff Hewell received a medical furlough and was still at home when Fort Donelson fell to Union troops. Jeff Hewell never returned to the regiment. (Emily and Ronnie Townes.)

Cherry J. White served in Capt. McKinney Dooley's Company of the 54th Tennessee Infantry Regiment. Confederate authorities consolidated the 54th with the 48th after Fort Donelson, and White's Company became Company C, 48th Tennessee. White does not appear on any muster rolls after the consolidation. (Emily and Ronnie Townes.)

Composed entirely of East Tennessee companies, the 61st Tennessee served in the brigade of John Crawford Vaughan (page 37). John King, from Hawkins County, served in Company E and fought in the defense of Vicksburg. Captured and exchanged after the fall of Vicksburg, Vaughan's brigade received horses and fought the rest of the war in East Tennessee, Western North Carolina, and Southwest Virginia. King deserted his regiment in March 1865 and returned home. (Emily and Ronnie Townes.)

Five

ARTILLERY, STAFF, CHAPLAINS, MARINES, AND SAILORS

There were two types of artillery during the Civil War—light and heavy. The light artillery (or field) was the most common, and these cannons traveled by way of horse-drawn caissons. Heavy artillery consisted of large, heavy cannons that were designed for defense of static installations, especially along the coasts or rivers. Occasionally, heavy artillerymen also manned heavy guns on field carriages for use in sieges. Tennessee raised both light and heavy artillery batteries (the basic unit for artillery). The light artillery served throughout the Confederacy, while the heavy artillery served on the Mississippi, Tennessee, and Cumberland Rivers. After the loss of these rivers to Union forces, Tennessee's heavy artillerymen manned guns at Vicksburg, Port Hudson, and Mobile, and some converted to light artillery.

Armies required a certain number of specialists to undertake production, acquisition, and the engineering of defenses, railroads, and bridge building. Likewise, commanders required staff officers to handle all sorts of tasks from clerking to repairing weapons and from managing wagon trains to securing rations. The frontline soldiers referred to these men as "yeller dogs" and considered them to be a privileged class that avoided combat. One soldier thought there to be more men on duty as staff officers than there were in the ranks. Despite the beliefs of the common soldiers, armies could not function without the labors of these men, and staff duty was no guarantee of safety. Gen. Joe Wheeler, for example, had 18 staff officers killed or wounded in the course of the war.

While staff officers saw to the feeding and equipping of the men, doctors and chaplains looked to their physical and moral health. Confederate chaplains hailed from various backgrounds; some were professional ministers while others received appointments from the ranks. During combat, these men assisted the doctors in the hospitals and carried news of the deceased to those at home.

The Confederates also maintained a very creative and daring, but small, naval force with a marine corps. Tennessee produced three Confederate States Marine Corps officers as well as navy personnel.

The most famous artillerist in the Western theater, John W. Morton, was 18 years old and a student at the Western Military Institute when the war began. Surrendered at Fort Donelson and exchanged, he served as General Forrest's chief of artillery. After the war, Morton briefly studied medicine before farming full time. He became the commissioner of agriculture and was the first state commander of the United Confederate Veterans. Morton was also active in the Ku Klux Klan until its dissolution in 1869. (TSM/THS.)

These Tennessee artillerymen pose around one of their field guns. Rutledge's Artillery formed in Nashville and dispatched to East Tennessee and reported to General Zollicoffer. The battery contained four 6-pounders and two howitzers and fought at Fishing Creek, Kentucky. The battery also fought at Shiloh, after which it consolidated with McClung's Battery. The consolidated unit fought in East Tennessee and Southwest Virginia from 1863 until the end of the war. (TSLA.)

Raford F. (left) and Benjamin F. Ammons (right) served with Company L, 1st Tennessee Heavy Artillery, at Island No. 10 in the Mississippi River. Most of the battery escaped to Memphis before the capitulation and then served at Vicksburg. Raford later joined Newsom's 18th Tennessee cavalry and lost an arm at Brice's Crossroads. Benjamin, crippled from an accident, never returned to the service. Both men lived in Hardeman County after the war. (TSLA.)

William Winston, a carpenter by trade, rose to command Keiter's Battery in late 1863. The battery thereafter was known as Winston's Battery. The unit manned an enormous 128-pound rifled gun at the Battle of Belmont, Missouri, in 1861 but surrendered with the Island No. 10 garrison in the spring of 1862. Exchanged, the battery served at various times with the Army of Tennessee, Forrest's cavalry corps, and in the defenses of Mobile. (TSLA.)

In 1861, 2nd Lt. Thomas B. Cook(e) joined the Confederate army. He was first commissioned as a lieutenant in Nelson's Artillery, and the unit served the large cannon with the 1st Tennessee Heavy Artillery as part of the Mississippi River defenses. Captured at Island No. 10, Cook spent several months as a prisoner of war at Johnson's Island until exchanged. He died during the fighting around Port Hudson, Louisiana, on May 27, 1863. (TSLA.)

Confederate armies required massive amounts of supplies to remain operational. The Department of Nitre and Mining worked tirelessly to locate domestic supplies of crucial materials for manufacturing. Memphian Lt. Col. William Richardson Hunt served in the Quartermaster and Artillery Department of the Bureau of Nitre and Mining and commanded the arsenal at Briarfield, Mississippi, for most of the war. He surrendered with Gen. Richard Taylor's Department of Alabama, Mississippi, and East Louisiana in 1865. (TSM.)

Samuel Lockett enjoyed a distinguished career in the Engineer Corps. Lockett graduated from the U.S. Military Academy in the class of 1854. He resigned his commission in 1861 and thereafter served as the chief engineer for Generals Pemberton, Johnston, Polk, Stewart, and Taylor. Engineers, among other things, designed defensive works, and Lockett laid out the Vicksburg defenses and Port Hudson defenses. At the end of the war, he was chief engineer in the Department of Alabama, Mississippi, and East Louisiana. (TSLA.)

James Linton Cooper served as a sergeant in Company C, 20th Tennessee Infantry Regiment. In July 1864, Cooper joined the staff of his brigade commander, Gen. John C. Tyler, as acting assistant inspector general and served as such until the end of the war. Cooper survived the war, but his close friend Capt. Tod Carter (page 88) did not. (Emily and Ronnie Townes.)

This image shows two staff officers with ancestral ties to two of the most powerful antebellum political families in Middle Tennessee. Lt. William Mecklenburg Polk (left) was the youngest son of Gen. Leonidas Polk (page 22), and Lt. Samuel Donelson (right) was the son of Gen. Daniel Smith Donelson (page 21). Both young men served on their respective father's staff during the war and served briefly together on General Polk's staff. Donelson later served as a staff officer to General Forrest alongside Forrest's son, William (page 66). (Bruce Holher.)

Five Ridley brothers from Rutherford County served in the Confederate army. George C. Ridley began the war as a lieutenant of Company F, 9th Tennessee Cavalry (Ward's/Bennett's). He later served as aide-de-camp and acting assistant inspector general for Gen. Benjamin J. Hill (page 33) of Forrest's cavalry corps. (Bruce Holher.)

Charles Lewis Ridley bore witness to the Battle of Murfreesboro as Union troops retreated through his family farm, and his house burned shortly after the battle. The youngest of the five brothers, Charles was too young to enlist, but Union troops arrested him on charges of bushwhacking and sentenced him to hang. The night before the execution, Forrest's cavalry swarmed into Murfreesboro and freed all of the prisoners. Thus saved, Charles joined the Confederate army as a volunteer aide-de-camp alongside his brother George. (Bruce Holher.)

Bromfield Lewis Ridley attended the Western Military Institute when the war began. As the Union army retreated through his farm on December 31, 1862, Bromfield and others captured a number of soldiers, including a colonel. He later joined Company F, 9th Tennessee Cavalry. Commissioned a lieutenant, he served on the staff of Gen. A. P. Stewart (page 23) from June 1863 until the surrender. After the war, Bromfield Ridley wrote *Battles and Sketches of the Army of Tennessee*. (Bruce Holher.)

Alex Vick attended Cumberland College before the war and joined the Lebanon Grays, which became part of the 7th Tennessee Infantry Regiment. Vick served as the regimental quartermaster until Robert Hatton (page 32) received promotion to brigadier general, after which Vick served as the brigade quartermaster and was promoted to major. He ended the war as chief quartermaster for Gen. A. P. Hill's corps in the Army of Northern Virginia. (TSM.)

Matthew Fontaine Maury, born in Virginia, grew up in Williamson County, Tennessee. Known as the "Pathfinder of the Seas," Commander Maury served in the U.S. Navy before the war. An injury kept him from sea service, and he dedicated his life to studying oceanographic geography, navigation, and meteorology and published the first book on oceanography. He served in the Confederate Navy until the end of the war, after which he taught at the Virginia Military Institute. (TSM.)

Henry Melville Doak enlisted in Company E, 19th Tennessee, and served as sergeant major. He received a commission in the Confederate States Marine Corps and served at Charleston, Drewry's Bluff, Savannah, and Wilmington. He commanded a battery at Fort Fisher and received a facial wound in the Union attack. Held briefly as a prisoner, he rejoined the Confederate Marines, fought at Sayler's Creek, and surrendered at Appomattox. He owned the *Nashville Banner* newspaper after the war. (TSLA.)

Eugene Robinett Smith served in the 2nd, 44th, and 25th Tennessee Infantry before joining the Confederate States Marine Corps in November 1864. He served at Drewry's Bluff and Charleston. Upon the evacuation of Charleston, Smith served in Virginia until his capture at Sayler's Creek on April 6, 1865. After the war, Smith practiced medicine. Upon his death in 1929, Smith was the last Confederate Marine officer to die, outliving Henry Doak by nearly six months. (Thomas Hammock and David Sullivan.)

Robert M. Ramsey, from East Tennessee, enlisted in the 1st Georgia Regulars in 1861. He received a commission in the Marines and served at Pensacola, Mobile, and Drewry's Bluff before being court martialed in July 1862, after which he served as a scout in East Tennessee. However, he was again court martialed. Charged with treason and murder after the war, Ramsey received a pardon and paid restitution but left Tennessee. He resettled in North Carolina and farmed until his death in 1890. (B. Ramsey Powell and David Sullivan.)

This image bears the following inscription on the reverse: "Dr. Samuel M. Gladney, surgeon of the Confederacy, 1861–1865." The photograph also carries the mark of a Knoxville photographer. Gladney began the war as an assistant surgeon in the 27th Mississippi Infantry Regiment and served in various hospitals within the Army of Tennessee. (TSM.)

Marion Townes was a native of Carroll County, Tennessee. With doctors in short supply, the Confederate War Department assigned Townes to the Trans-Mississippi Army. He survived the war and lived out his life in Texas. (Emily and Ronnie Townes.)

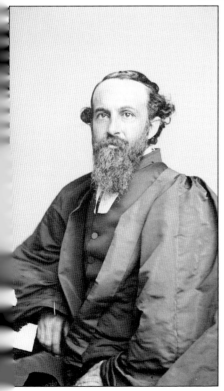

Bishop Charles Todd Quintard was both a doctor and Episcopal minister. He served his congregation as the chaplain of the Rock City Guards and the 1st Tennessee Infantry. During battle, Quintard worked in the hospitals and put his ministerial and medical training to use. After the war, he was the archbishop of Tennessee and was instrumental in reestablishing the University of the South at Sewanee, Tennessee. (LOC.)

Dr. C. D. Elliott operated the Nashville Female Academy. As regiments passed through Nashville headed to the front, Dr. Elliott often fed the men on the academy's grounds, with his students serving the tables. Many of the soldiers knew Dr. Elliott from their sisters and sweethearts receiving their education at his school. Dr. Elliott later joined these men as chaplain for Maney's Brigade. (TSLA.)

Stephen Chastain Talley grew up in Sumner County and joined the Methodist Church. In 1852, he joined the Missionary Baptist Church and began preaching. He served as a private in the 2nd Tennessee Cavalry until June 1862, when Colonel Barteau appointed him chaplain. The battle of Harrisburg, Mississippi, cost the regiment nearly 60 men, and General Forrest sent Talley to carry the news to the families. Captured and charged with spying, he remained a prisoner of war until late in the war. (TSM/THS.)

Six

THE LEGACY

The surrender of Robert E. Lee's army at Appomattox in April 1865 was not the end of the war. While a few Tennessee regiments surrendered in Virginia, that vast majority of Tennessee troops surrendered in North Carolina as part of the Army of Tennessee. Other Tennessee troops, especially the cavalry serving with General Forrest, surrendered in Alabama. As the troops returned home, they realized that their world had changed. Many of these former soldiers had been on top of the social, economic, and political ladder before the war. They returned home to find their state ravaged by warfare, their homes destroyed, and even their families dispersed. With the Reconstruction plan imposed by the Union, many could no longer hold political office or even vote. The presence of recently freed blacks and occupation troops, the economic depression, the upheaval of Southern society, and the vindictive nature of the Reconstruction state government left the Confederate veterans to ponder the terrible cost for a cause that failed.

Denied the right to vote or to strike back at Gov. William Brownlow's policies, some veterans formed the Ku Klux Klan in Pulaski, Tennessee, in 1866. This secret organization grew to other states and used fear and intimidation to hold onto the social order. Former soldiers like Gordon, Forrest, and Morton participated in the organization's activities. However, with the resignation of Reconstruction governor William Brownlow in 1869, Grand Wizard Nathan Bedford Forrest ordered the organization dissolved. Its reappearance in 1915 was not connected to the original organization.

As the veterans aged and the painful memories of the war and Reconstruction faded, the various regiments held reunions and began to erect markers and monuments and to mark graves. While Tennessee was the last state to leave the Union and the first state to return, it ironically became the central point of the two dominant Confederate heritage organizations. Both the United Confederate Veterans and the United Daughters of the Confederacy started in Nashville. This tradition holds true today in that the Sons of Confederate Veterans headquarters remains in Columbia, Tennessee.

Started as a social club in Pulaski by former soldiers, the Ku Klux Klan evolved into a secret, armed, vigilante organization that maintained control of the freedmen and hampered the efforts of the Reconstruction government using fear, intimidation, and beatings. This photograph is one of the earliest known of a Klansman. At this time, the robes were not white but actually colorful. The Klan flag seen in this photograph survives in the Tennessee State Museum Collection. (TSM/THS.)

In the years after the war, Southerners sought to cope with the reality of defeat and looked for heroic figures that symbolized Southern virtue and bravery. Images of Robert E. Lee reached unrivaled popularity. The reunion photographic album of Barteau's 2nd Tennessee Cavalry and Morton's Battery, two units that never fought under Lee, contained this rare postwar version of the famous Confederate general. (TSM/THS.)

After the war, Gen. William Hicks Jackson (page 34) turned Belle Meade Plantation into a world-class center for raising Thoroughbred horses. In this photograph, taken at Belle Meade, Jackson (left) talks with his old West Point classmate and former Confederate cavalry general Fitzhugh Lee, nephew of Robert E. Lee. Undoubtedly, they not only discussed horses but also swapped war stories. Jackson fought under Wheeler and Forrest, while Lee fought under J. E. B. Stuart and Wade Hampton. (TSLA.)

Arthur Hopkins Beard, a native of Madison County, Alabama, served in Russell's 4th Alabama Cavalry as a lieutenant. Russell's regiment contained many Tennesseans, and Jeffery Forrest, brother of General Forrest, served as colonel. Beard resigned his commission in October 1863 due to the amputation of his arm from wounds received at Parker's Crossroads, Tennessee, in December 1862. After the war, Beard raised cotton in Arkansas, but he lived the last 20 years of his life in Memphis. (TSM.)

The Civil War cost thousands upon thousands of American lives. Even greater than those killed were the numbers of those physically, mentally, or emotionally scarred by the horrors of a Civil War battlefield. Capt. Henley Fugate served in Company A, 63rd Tennessee, and lost his left arm at Chickamauga. He appears in this postwar photograph with his wife. His missing arm is plainly visible. (Emily and Ronnie Townes.)

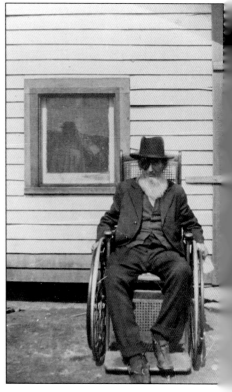

Christopher Green served in the 53rd Tennessee Infantry and was absent without leave in 1862. He appears to be confined to a wheelchair at the time of this photograph. Tennessee Confederate soldiers and their spouses were eligible to receive pensions if their records indicated that they had not deserted or taken the oath of allegiance before April 1865. (TSLA.)

The Civil War left thousands of veterans with poor health, and many faced financial strain during the postwar era. In 1889, the Tennessee General Assembly passed legislation for the construction of a home for indigent and disabled Confederate veterans on the grounds of the Hermitage. The soldier's home opened in 1892 and served nearly 700 veterans in its 41 years of operation. The Soldier's Home Cemetery contains the remains of 487 former Confederates. (Ladies Hermitage Association.)

This photograph shows the McGavock Confederate Cemetery, which is located at Carnton Plantation. The Battle of Franklin left thousands of dead soldiers. Many of the Confederates were removed from the battlefield and reinterred to this cemetery thanks to the efforts of Carrie McGavock. Southern women, many of them daughters of Confederate soldiers, began to mark and locate the graves of fallen Confederates. These efforts gave rise to the United Daughters of the Confederacy. (TSM.)

Caroline Douglas Meriwether Goodlett is credited as being the founder of the United Daughters of the Confederacy. After the war, Goodlett moved from Kentucky to Nashville and married a Tennessee Confederate veteran. She formed a benevolent society to purchase artificial limbs for veterans and raised money for the Confederate Veterans Home. Eventually, Goodlett's charitable works grew into a national organization, which was known as the United Daughters of the Confederacy by 1895. (TSM/THS.)

The veterans began to form a national organization in 1889. Sumner Archibald Cunningham, a former member of the 41st Tennessee Infantry, founded *Confederate Veteran* magazine in 1893 and served as the editor until his death in 1913. The magazine published obituaries, accounts of the war, and reunion announcements and was the voice of the United Confederate Veterans (UCV). In this portrait, painted by Cornelius Hankins between 1906 and 1914, he is wearing a medal presented to him by the UCV for his work. (TSM.)

Read from Left to Right.
Top Row___ Azariah H Hancock, J Wm Bowden, Paul R Orr, J Watt Allen, Jack Coleman,
Alex H Lankford, and M M Doc Critchfield.
Bottom Row: Col Jones, Robt Diggs, Gus Harris, Dr Felix Porter, J Polk Peoples, Jno S Orr
Jas P Copper, Jno J Thompson, Jno D Looney, R Pink Kirby, W Devernagh Kendall, Asst.
Sam A Miller, Frank M Bells, G Wash Swor, Jas R Daniels, Rufe B Oliva, Willis L Hagler (Bud
Tobe Porter and Joe Warren were colored cooks, not enlisted.

This undated photograph taken around the Confederate monument in Paris, Henry County, shows the surviving members of the 5th Tennessee Infantry Regiment. Visible on the right of the first row are two of the African American cooks who accompanied the regiment during the war. Pictured on the extreme left is Gov. James David Porter of Henry County, who served as a staff officer for Gen. Benjamin Franklin Cheatham (page 25) throughout the war. (Paris–Henry County Museum.)

Veterans organizations often carried military names such as bivouac or company. Company B of United Confederate Veterans was centered in Nashville. These veterans companies often used military terms for the leaders. This gives rise to confusion, as some soldiers may have been called captain, major, or colonel based on their veteran "rank," while their real rank in the Confederate army may have simply been "private." (TSM.)

As the United Confederate Veterans organization grew, national reunions were held across the South and occasionally in conjunction with the Grand Army of the Republic, the Union veterans' organization. This photograph shows the attendees from the Forrest Camp of Nashville at the reunion in Washington, D.C., in 1914. If these men could have reached Washington during the war, things might have turned out differently. (LOC.)

While thousands often attended the national reunions, the unit reunions offered veterans a chance to see their old comrades in a much smaller and relaxed atmosphere. This photograph was taken at one of the reunions of the 24th Tennessee Infantry Regiment. They pose with one of the flags they bravely defended in four years of brutal warfare. (TSM.)

As the memories of the war faded and the sections of the country attempted to heal the wounds of the war, captured battle flags were often returned to the states from which they were taken during the war. This photograph from around the time of World War I shows the Illinois Congressional delegation as they return the flag of the 11th Tennessee Infantry. (LOC.)

The veterans organizations as well as the United Daughters of the Confederacy often raised funds for constructing monuments to commemorate the heroism of Confederate soldiers. The bronze statue seen here of Gen. Nathan Bedford Forrest stands over the grave of the general in Memphis. The photograph dates to the 1905 dedication ceremony. This statue as well as other Confederate symbols, such as the battle flag, remain hotly debated issues, reminding many that the war is still controversial and in the collective memory. (LOC.)

The man on the right is M. W. McKnight of Company C, 2nd Tennessee Cavalry (Barteau's), while the man on the left is tentatively identified as either W. B. Willard or A. B. McKnight, both of Company C. The men appear in their distinctive UCV uniforms. The 2nd created a unit photograph album to take to reunions. The album survives in the collection of the Tennessee Historical Society at the Tennessee State Museum. (TSM/THS.)

George F. Hager served as lieutenant in Company G, 2nd Tennessee Cavalry (Barteau's). After the war, Hager wrote the regimental history for *Military Annals of Tennessee*, assisted in the publication of *Hancock's Diary: or, a History of the Second Tennessee Cavalry*, and assembled a photographic album. Many of the photographs from the album appear throughout the text. (TSM/THS.)

Confederate veteran John B. Kennedy posed for this photograph with the war-torn remnants of his regiment's battle flag. Also visible is his canteen, on which he painted a likeness of the flag. The material culture of the war remains a powerful tool for interpreting the experience of Civil War Tennesseans. The Tennessee State Museum holds over 60 Confederate flags as well as uniforms, weapons, and equipment and actively seeks donations for their conservation. (TSLA.)

"If only we had these at Shiloh." Perhaps these are thoughts going through the mind of Harry Rene Lee as he contemplates this military aircraft. Lee served as the commander of the United Confederate Veterans from 1935 to 1936. Many soldiers took their first train ride when they enlisted in 1861. By the time the last veterans died in the early 1950s, jet planes were screeching across the sky. (TSLA.)

Discover Thousands of Local History Books
Featuring Millions of Vintage Images

Arcadia Publishing, the leading local history publisher in the United States, is committed to making history accessible and meaningful through publishing books that celebrate and preserve the heritage of America's people and places.

Find more books like this at
www.arcadiapublishing.com

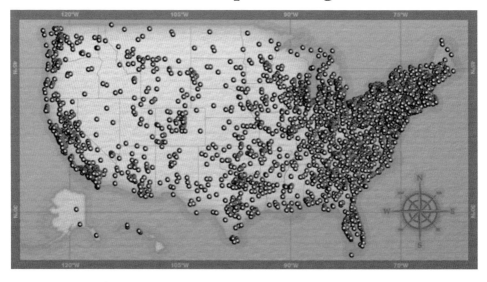

Search for your hometown history, your old stomping grounds, and even your favorite sports team.

Consistent with our mission to preserve history on a local level, this book was printed in South Carolina on American-made paper and manufactured entirely in the United States. Products carrying the accredited Forest Stewardship Council (FSC) label are printed on 100 percent FSC-certified paper.

MADE IN THE